Adventure Sports

SURFING

Adventure Sports
SURFING

JOHN CONWAY

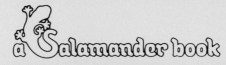

a Salamander book

Published by Salamander Books Limited
LONDON • NEW YORK

A SALAMANDER BOOK

©1988 Salamander Books Ltd.,
129/137 York Way,
London N7 9LG,
United Kingdom.

ISBN 0 86101 361 1

Editor: Terence Monaighan
Designed by Wavelength Magazine
Colour reproductions: Melbourne Graphics Ltd.
Filmset: SX Composing Ltd.
Printed in China

The author
John Conway has been involved with the sport of surfing for twenty-five years. While a surfer and surfing photographer he established one of Britain's first customised surfboard factories in the early 1970s. In 1978 he founded *Atlantic Surfer* (now *Surf Scene*), Europe's first colour surfing magazine. As a contest director and tournament organiser, John has been responsible for the first world ranked event to be staged in Europe – The 1981 Gul/Alder Euro-Pro. He was also the contest director of the first ASP World Tour event to be staged in Europe, The 1983 Fosters Draught Euro-Pro, and the richest Pro-Am ever staged in Europe – The Watergate Euro-Pro. John Conway is now the publishing editor of the international surfing magazine *Wavelength*. He is still actively involved in the sport both as a surfer and is also acknowledged as one of Europe's leading water sport photographers.

The illustrator
Simon Evans studied illustration at Cornwall College of Further and Higher Education, qualifying in 1983. Since then, he has travelled around the world to surf in Europe, Australia, Bali and Sri Lanka. Now resident in Falmouth, Cornwall, Simon works as a freelance designer and illustrator for a number of publications while still taking every opportunity to continue surfing.

CONTENTS

INTRODUCTION

Why do men bother to climb mountains, canoe rapids, free-fall parachute, hang glide, or participate in many other high-risk sports? I have only one answer and that is "thrill". The feeling of adrenalin coursing through the body that accompanies the surviving of a dangerous act. In the case of surfing, just picture the mountain of pure indigo marching majestically landward. An ocean swell, caused by a cyclonic storm many thousands of miles out at sea, has but a few seconds of life left. It becomes bigger and more awesome as it erupts into a solid wall of water, pitching upwards in front of an off-shore wind. The surfer arcs white plumes across the wall of water, until, in its last few seconds of life, the wave rebukes the intruder, opens up its jaws, and pitches out over him, consuming him under tons of water!

The ultimate and most dangerous place to ride a wave is deep inside the tube. This is one end of the scale with its danger and thrills. The sport has many players, ranging from those who rise to the challenge of riding "Pipeline" in Hawaii, to the recreational surfer. Don't make the assumption that surfing is just for the young. The sport can be enjoyed by all, no matter what age or sex. Anybody can have fun in the surf learning to ride a surfboard. There is no better feeling on earth than spending a sunny summer at the beach with a bunch of friends, a new surfboard, an off-shore wind, and a clean summer swell, while enjoying the thrill of riding waves.

Like any other adventure sport, surfing has an element of danger and has to be approached in a reasonable manner. If you were contemplating taking up mountaineering, for instance, it would be foolish to buy a length of rope, a pair of climbing boots and a ticket to Tibet! The same applies to surfing. Waves are created by powerful storms. Those nice neat lines of surf that roll gently into the beach hold hidden dangers beneath the surface.

Through the book there rests an underlying theme: safety and the awareness of other surfers. Once this code of conduct becomes second nature and you have mastered the basic skills of the sport, the door to the world of surfing, travelling and competing is open to you.

If you are not a competent swimmer (and by competent I don't mean with the ability to casually breast-stroke a few gentle lengths of a pool), it is totally irresponsible of you to con-template taking a surfboard into the sea. Swimming in the surf against breaking waves and undercurrents is a far cry from the safety of a swimming pool. I have seen many surfers rescued by the Lifeguard Service, apart from those who have been hit and injured by their surfboards. Most have been novices who were not strong enough swimmers and did not have a clue how to handle themselves in an emergency in the surf. If you want to learn to surf and your level of swimming proficiency is low or lapsed, then get down to your local swimming pool to improve your swimming under supervision. Remember, water safety, personal survival, and a good swimming standard, are the best insurance policies you can have.

It would seem that when the divine hand of creation made planet earth, surfing got a particularly good deal. It really cannot be coincidence that 99 percent of the world's best surfing locations are situated in the most exotic parts of the planet, and I don't think you'll hear many surfers complaining about it. With this backdrop who can blame participants in the sport making surfing a lifestyle?

At a certain level of competence, surfers take one of two routes and become either competitors chasing the dream of the elusive ASP World Crown, or they are caught by the lust to wander the oceans of the world. Whether as a competitor or traveller, life for these people is unlikely to be the same again. However, for the majority of social and recreational surfers, the bug will not bite that deep and so the sport is largely made up of weekend recreational surfers.

This book has been written to explain surfing for all levels. For the beginner, when the frustrations of spending most of a a surfing session on the sea bed get too much, step-by-step diagrams will iron out the problems. Certain technical words in the text are highlighted in bold; they are explained in more detail in the glossary (page 123).

CHAPTER 1

BEACH SAFETY

Before even attempting to learn to surf it is important to establish the "ground rules" of beach safety. A beginner to the sport falls into the category of being a "bather armed with a surfboard". A beachgoer attempting to surf for the first time will do the same as people worldwide. First, he or she will lay down a towel or beach mat to stake a territorial claim to a piece of sand. Second, strip off. Third, pick up the surfboard and rush down to the water's edge. And fourth, run into the breaking waves. It may be cruel to categorize people this way, but a surfboard in the hands of an inexperienced person is potentially dangerous. In breaking waves, a beginner has a hard enough task even holding on to and protecting themselves from their board.

At this point a bather becomes a surfer and carrying a board means being confronted by a whole new world of flags, signs, discs and buoys. Getting things wrong means he or she will become the focus of attention for the whole beach as the lifeguard singles them out for a vast amount of verbal abuse. Surfers and bathers do not mix. So, what do you do on your first surfing session, and how does the beach system work?

CLOSED. This rule applies to surfers and bathers alike. If in the lifeguard's opinion, the beach is unsafe for the general public he will close the beach and prevent both surfers and bathers from entering the water. Some beaches are protected from the open ocean swell by reefs, headlands and other land masses, so they are classified as "safe", and very rarely need to be closed to the public. However, because waves do not break on them (apart from during the occasional heavy storm) they are of no use for surfing. The only dangers encountered might be stubbing your toe on a sand-covered rock, or getting stung by something nasty in the water!

Lifeguards around the world patrol surf beaches to protect the public. The Lifeguard Service operates on a prevention rather than cure philosophy and in order to eliminate as many dangerous problems as possible they segregate surfers from bathers. There are several methods of doing this, the commonest being a partial or complete ban on surfing on bathing beaches, or for bathers and surfers to have separate areas on the beach. Areas are clearly marked by flags, signs, buoys and by constantly announced reminders from

OPEN AND CLOSED BEACHES

The red-flag system is used worldwide to indicate whether or not the beach is open or closed. A red flag indicates DANGER BEACH

Right: Lifeguards keep a constant eye on the areas. Make sure you surf in the correct area of the beach. If you do not know or are unsure ask the lifeguards where you can surf.

BASIC BEACH SAFETY RULES

The flag and disc systems may vary from country to country but the colours are now generally accepted worldwide.

If you are confused or do not understand the local beach safety system:
- Do not enter the water.
- Ask the lifeguard; he will tell you where or where not to surf.

- If the lifeguard tells you the beach is closed (Red Flag) ask him when the beach will be open again, or
- Ask him to advise on another beach in the area that will be open and safe.
- Red and Yellow Discs or flags – Bathing area, no surfers.
- Black and White discs or flags – Surfing area, no bathing.

the patrolling lifeguards. A lifeguard's first responsibility is for the safety of the bather, and the area the lifeguard sets aside for bathing has precedence over the area set aside for surfing. To protect the general public from loose surfboards, the two areas are usually split by buoy lines running out to sea, or by a no-man's land.

You may think the lifeguards are over-cautious and the beach looks perfectly safe. However, they patrol that stretch of beach and know every hidden danger and it is their responsibility not only to save life but to protect it, so if you are told the beach is closed you must accept this. In some countries, if a surfer ignores the beach area system he or she runs the risk of having their board confiscated for a considerable length of time, while surfing on a non-surfing beach can mean being arrested and fined.

UNPATROLLED AND UNMARKED BEACHES

The advice above is sound if you live in or visit a coastal area with an established beach area system for surfers and bathers, but what do you do if none of this applies? Unlike bathing, surfing doesn't have a closed season. Wetsuits are worn by surfers to overcome the discomfort of cold water, so the sport can be carried on all year round. It would be impractical to advise someone

Right: Lifeguards keep a constant eye on the areas. Make sure you surf in the correct area. If you do not know ask the lifeguards where you can surf to avoid endangering anyone.

Below: The bathing area is marked with a red and yellow flag or discs. The surfing area is marked with black and white flags or discs. Areas of danger are marked with red flags. The red flag means that in the opinion of the lifeguards the beach is unsafe for bathing or surfing. Never enter the water when the red flag is flying. If you are ever in doubt about the safe areas consult the lifeguard.

BEACH SAFETY AREAS

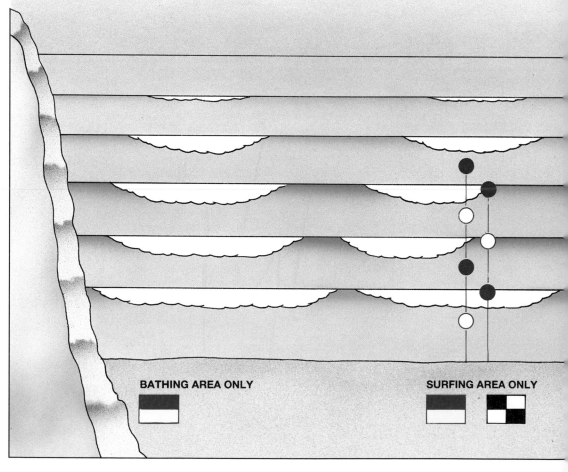

BATHING AREA ONLY

SURFING AREA ONLY

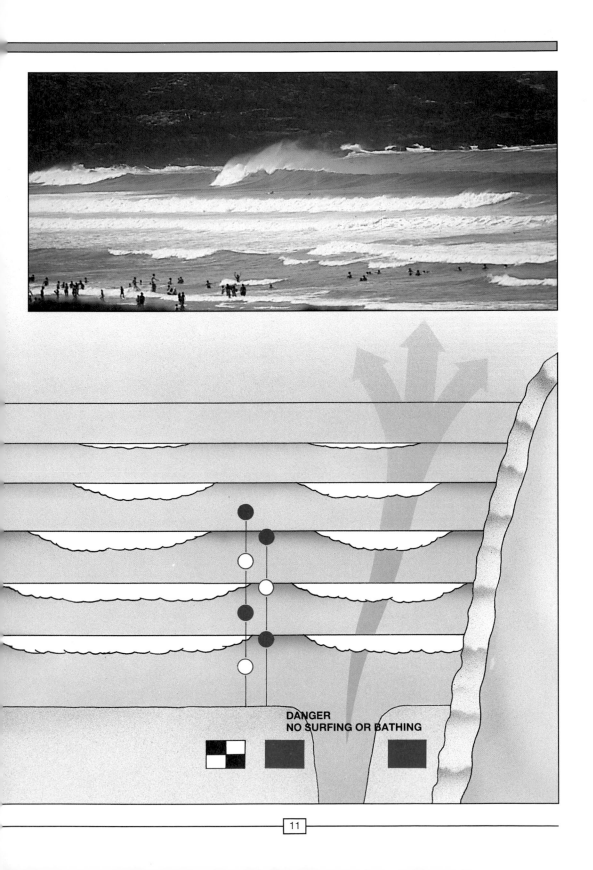

DANGER
NO SURFING OR BATHING

who is seriously learning to surf to give it up until the lifeguards are back on the beach next season, or not to surf for the winter.

If the area you live in or regularly visit has a surf club, or even a surf life-saving club, join it. If there is no such club in the area then enlist the help of local, proficient surfers to keep an eye on you. Never go in the water alone.

On unpatrolled beaches always surf with friends and stay within shouting distance. If you have any reservations about sea conditions don't go surfing. If the undercurrents make it hard to keep your feet, come out of the water.

The importance of the above points cannot be overemphasized. After all, how are you going to learn to surf if you can only go in when it is considered perfectly safe? Once you can read and understand the condition of the sea and its dangers

you will realise just how foolhardy it could have been to ignore these warnings.

Until you can handle a surfboard with some degree of control, treat the sea with the attitude that it is waiting to capitalise on your mistakes every time you surf.

SURFING SCHOOLS, INSTRUCTION, AND TRY BEFORE YOU BUY

To avoid putting yourself at risk get instruction through a surf shop or surf school. There are advantages. First and foremost, a qualified surfer or ex-lifesaver will be looking after your personal safety along with a group of other beginners. You will be taught thoroughly and made to observe the beach safety code. Individuals with hire boards are considered a liability by lifeguards, and

when the surfing area becomes crowded they often shut off the area. Lifeguards are more likely to allow a supervised group to carry on surfing.

Not everyone takes to surfing, so if you hire a surfboard and have a hard time it may very well put you off the sport. Under supervision a surfing instructor will help you do things correctly when you seem to be spending all your time in the water. You will be taught the basics of surfboard control from this point and, if you decide that surfing is for you, your instructor will be able to advise you on how and where to buy your first board, and which are the best beaches to learn to surf.

It is also a good idea to get help on a one-to-one basis from either an instructor or a good surfer. An experienced pair of eyes may instantly solve a problem you may have been battling with for hours.

BEGINNER AND EXPERT ZONES

BEGINNER'S AREA

Below: This shows clearly the way the waves break from the peak either left or right. A wave will break when the angle of the beach contour changes beneath it. Beach breaks are subject to constant movement due to storms and large wave action. The banks of sand that cause waves to break will also change their characteristics with movement.

Before a storm a beach break could be a perfectly hollow, pitching wave; after the storm with the banks destroyed the wave may disappear completely or the bank could be partially damaged and collapse. This makes the wave break in deeper water, it will become full and sluggish. A reef or point break with a solid bottom does not suffer from such drastic changes of character.

**EXPERIENCED AND
ADVANCED AREA**

**DANGER
RIP CURRENT**

CHAPTER 2

BASIC EQUIPMENT

Today's foam and fibreglass surfboards stand tribute to over 30 years of development. Back in the early 1950s a technique of bonding fibreglass matting to polyurethane foam with polyester resin was perfected in California, with much of the credit going to the late Bob Simmons. Prior to this, shapers worked with solid balsa wood which is much heavier than foam and when it became damaged it soaked up water and rotted away.

Today, these early foam and fibreglass boards would now be considered "logs", weighing 30 to 40 pounds (15 to 20 kilos). Surfboards remained around 9 feet 6 inches (3 metres) long until 1965 when a young Australian, Bob McTavish, came up with a radical new design, the V-bottom. This made surfboards much shorter and far more manoeuverable, beginning an era of change that saw the length of boards drop from 9 feet 6 inches to 5 feet 6 inches (2 metres). Surfing technique was far different in the era of the longer surfboards, with surfers having to be strong enough to paddle the massive hulk through breaking waves. If he or she lost their board either on the way out or when riding, it became necessary to swim all the way to the beach to retrieve it. A leash would possibly not have been practical because of the sheer volume and weight of the board. A surfer would probably have had a leg pulled out of its socket on a heavy wipe-out!

Today, surfers have the luxury of lightweight surfboards, leashes and wetsuits. With the development of equipment has come a much greater choice, which in turn can lead to confusion when a new surfer is confronted with a shop full of surfboards, wetsuits and accessories. The basic item of equipment you need to learn to surf with is obvious-

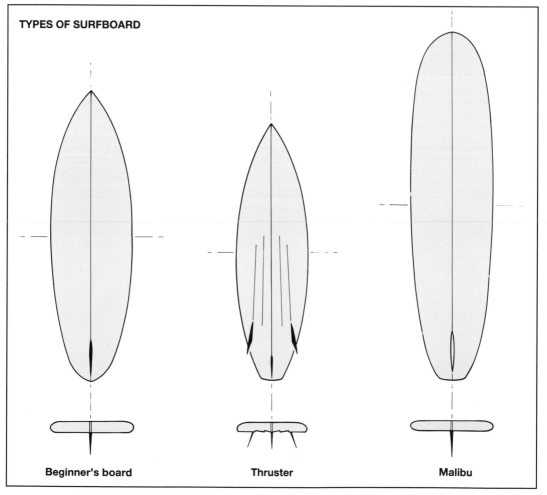

TYPES OF SURFBOARD

Beginner's board   Thruster   Malibu

ly the surfboard. Other essential items are a block of wax, a pair of trunks (recommended to protect against wax rash) and a leash. Where you surf and what time of the year you intend to take up the sport will dictate the necessity for a wetsuit.

SURFBOARDS

A **blank** or core of polyurethane foam forms the heart of a surfboard. These are manufactured in different lengths and widths and usually have a thin strip of balsa wood in the middle, known as the **stringer**, to give the blank strength and rigidity. A **shaper** hand crafts the rough blank into a finished form. This is the most skilled job in a surfboard factory and very often shapers are skilled surfers capable of transferring their knowledge of surfing into a highly-functional surfboard. The blank is marked and cut out using a template, known as the **plan shape**, and then planed with an electric planer to remove the rough outer skin. Using the planer, the bottom and deck contour are shaped into the blank. The **rails**, or edges, are cut in with the planer and the board is then finished by hand with sandpaper blocks.

Once the blank is finished the airbrush artist is able to spray on a design using cellulose paints. Surfboards can be customised in this way to the purchaser's own specifications for an extra charge. A sprayed-on design is not a functional part of the surfboard; it is purely cosmetic and obviously won't make you surf any better.

Next, the sprayed blank is laminated with a hard coat of fibreglass to protect the fragile foam. Once the board is laminated and cured it is sanded to take off all the sharp fibreglass swarth. This has to be done extremely carefully so as not to sand through the hard fibreglass shell.

Surfboards can also be moulded. The same process is carried out to make a master or plug, then a mould is cast around the plug. Foam poured into the mould produces identical clones of the original.

The process of learning to surf is made much easier if you choose the right equipment. From the start, think of a surfboard as a platform to ride waves on. Surfboards for beginners, unlike those for experts, have to be longer, wider and thicker. Unfortunately, there is no formula or calculation that can be applied to determine the ideal length, width and thickness of surfboards for a person's bodyweight or level of experience. Your choice of equipment will determine how quickly you master the basics of paddling, balance and standing up.

Surfboards come in all shapes and sizes and, like golf clubs, they are designed for a specific task. A beginner's board, depending on the body weight of the individual, varies from 6 feet 6 inches to 8 feet (2-2.5

Above: The very basic equipment needed to learn to surf. A moulded surfboard, leash and a pair of shorts.

metres) in length, 22 inches (55 centimetres) wide and 3 inches (10 centimetres) to 3½ inches thick. The plan or outline shape has to be wider in the nose and tail in order to provide a stable platform. Mastering the basics of surfing is much easier on a stable, high flotation platform than on a narrow, unstable sinker. A beginner's board may not look as sleek as the shorter, expert models, but you will master the basics of surfing a lot sooner.

The amount of money you have to spend dictates the type of board you can buy. It is important to be aware of the options that are best suited to the basics of learning to surf. Look carefully at custom surfboards, moulded surfboards, and secondhand surfboards. Don't allow yourself to be talked into buying a surfboard just for the sake of getting into the water quickly, or because it looks like a super deal. A custom or hand-made board costs more than a moulded, mass-produced board, but for taking elementary steps in surfing, either board is adequate. Custom boards are tailor-made to your requirements and much lighter than moulded boards. This makes them more susceptible to **dings** (holes that puncture the outer fibreglass skin). Moulded boards are standard, manufactured models of various lengths, widths, and thicknesses, constructed from glassfibre reinforced plastic (GRP)and made in a two-part mould. They are tougher and will stand the many **wipe-outs** (falling off) that beginners will experience while mastering the basics of surfing. To help you decide which type of board to buy, it is important to look at custom and moulded boards in more detail.

CUSTOM BOARDS

Buying a custom surfboard starts with your first visit to the factory or surfshop where you will receive expert help ordering a board. If possible it is always better to go to the factory to talk to the person who will actually shape your board. He will want to know your weight, height, and level of ability. With these details he can then offer his opinion on the plan shape, length, width and thickness you require. This method of ordering a surfboard is used by surfers of all abilities right up to the top professionals.

Once you have established all the dimensions you can then choose the colour scheme. It is a bit like buying a new car, all the add-on extras cost, so keep it simple. If you learn quickly to master the basic skills on your beginner board it won't be too long before you want to trade in this basic model for something a little more advanced, and the hideous spray job you consider to

be state of the art may completely turn off someone else. In my experience, beginners do not want to draw attention to themselves so they usually order fairly plain, unassuming spray jobs. The colour of your board will not help you to learn to surf and it does not make the board function any better.

When placing a custom order, you will be asked how many fins you require on the board. Advanced board shapes with different fin configurations definitely perform better where experts are concerned, but with your first board going in a straight, controlled line is the first step, and one single, central fin adequately manages this task.

With your custom board ordered you have to sit back and wait for it to be hand-built. For the impatient, surfboard factories provide off-the-shelf **stock** custom boards. The larger surfboard factories have a showroom full of boards of all different shapes, lengths, and colours, which have been totally hand-built in exactly the same way as any other custom board. One of these off-the-peg boards may seem to fulfill all your requirements but I think it is very important to have a board tailor-made for your height, weight and level of skill. Alternatively, you may wish to buy a a moulded board.

MOULDED BOARDS

These boards are made as models. For example, a 6 feet 8 inch by 22 inches by 3½ inches (2 metres by 55 centimetres by 10 centimetres) rounded-area pintail with a single fin would be identical to the one before that came out of the mould and the one after. The method of construction is totally different to custom-built surfboards. Surfboard factories closely monitor the retail market and set trends by producing models for a specific group of purchasers. The 6 feet 8 inch area pintail surfboard is considered ideal for beginners to learn on. This model is aimed at individual beginners and at companies who require hire boards to rent out, such as surfing schools or surfshops. As these are lucrative markets a lot of time, money, and effort is spent on getting the board

right. A Research and Development Programme is responsible for the plan, or outline shape, and the length, width and thickness. These dimensions are passed on to a custom shaper who shapes the master model or **plug** for the moulder. This board is identical to a custom-shaped surfboard, the only difference being that a mould is cast around this master model. The cost per item is drastically reduced once the initial tooling costs have been recouped and the saving is then passed on to the consumer. The only slight disadvantage to the fashion-conscious is that each board is exactly the same, with only a slight cosmetic difference in colour designs. However, for the purpose of a platform to learn the

basics of surfing on it is perfectly adequate and the savings made here may allow for money to be spent later on a wetsuit. If your budget does not stretch to either a new custom or moulded board, then you could consider a secondhand or used surfboard. Remember, lots of people have learnt to surf before you and there is a chance that you can pick up a good secondhand custom or moulded surfboard.

Left: A good example of a custom-made surfboard seen worldwide.

Below: A fairly typical range of moulded boards of various sizes for varying levels of skill.

SECONDHAND BOARDS

When purchasing a secondhand board there are a few points to look out for. Make sure that the deck around the tail to the midway point is not spongey or delaminated, as this is caused by excessive use or bad original manufacture. What in fact happens is that the core or foam blank becomes compressed and the hard outer fibreglass shell breaks away from the foam. This is made even worse if the board has been badly dinged in the deck area because the foam core will soak up water like a sponge and further aggravate the problem. There is no satisfactory way to repair a board with bad deck delamination. If resin is pumped in to fill the cavity between the deck and the foam, the board weight is increased and its riding characteristics change.

Other points to watch out for are badly repaired dings, and loose fins. A surfboard with a finbox can be a problem; check by moving the fin from side to side that the box is not loose and look for water oozing out from around the sides of the box where it is fixed into the board.

It would be wise if you are going to buy a secondhand board to ask a competent surfer to advise you on the board you are contemplating buying. A reputable surf shop will always try to advise you on the best buy, but it will not do any harm to have independent second opinions on your intended purchase.

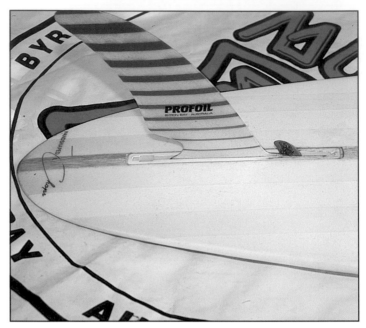

ACCESSORIES

Once you have chosen your surfboard you have to get it to the beach and protect it from damage. At the time of purchasing your board try to get a protective bag and the rest of the equipment such as a leash, rail saver and wax at an all-inclusive price. Below are what I consider to be the essential accessories for a complete beginner.

Leashes

Having bought a board the last thing you want is to lose it and get a ding in it while surfing or have the fin knocked off, so a leash is a very important accessory. This works very simply with one end attached to the board in a deck plug, the other to your ankle by a Velcro strap. The leash, depending on its manufacturer, is constructed of a length of solid urethane, approximately 6 to 7 feet long and ¼ inch (2 metres by 60 millimetres) thick. Urethane has an elastic property that allows it to repeatedly stretch and return to its original length.

When a surfer becomes separated from his or her board the wave will carry the board along with it until the elastic property of the leash reaches its maximum length of travel. It then starts to recoil to its original length and the board returns to its rider. To stop the hard urethane cutting into the rail of the board, make sure the leash has a webbing rail saver.

Wax

This is used on the deck of the board to give grip. It stops your feet slipping on the highly glossy finish of the surfboard.

There are many varieties, each for different weather conditions and ease of application. It also comes in a variety of different fragrances – the smell is not important but the climatic choice is. A thin layer of wax

Above: Normally fins are secured to the box with a screw. The screw can work loose and drop out when the surfboard has been used for some time. A foil clip has been invented to solve this problem.

should be rubbed onto the deck. A thick application of wax will not help you to stay on the board any more than a thin one. A coating of wax that has been applied too liberally will soften in the sun and pick up sand and grit from the beach. This accumulation will act as an abrasive surface against your skin, causing wax rash to the stomach and inside of the thighs. It also gets into cuts on the feet, turning them septic. It is much better to apply a thin coat before a surf session or use a wax comb to rough up the existing coat. The wax should be periodically removed with a wax comb.

Right: A custom surfboard starts life as a solid block of foam or blank. First, the shaper must cut away the surplus foam with an electric planer and then finish the job by hand.

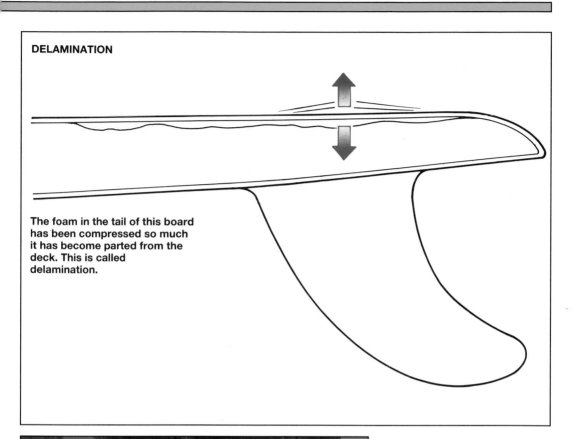

DELAMINATION

The foam in the tail of this board
has been compressed so much
it has become parted from the
deck. This is called
delamination.

Protective board bag

Surfboards are laminated with fibre-glass. This light but durable skin will under normal use withstand quite hard knocks, but it will easily puncture when it comes into contact with sharp objects such as the end of a car roof rack.

Surfboards bags are made to offer varying levels of protection to a surfboard. Some give little protection, these are called board socks. They are only used to protect against light knocks and scratches from everyday use.

Heavy airline-proof nylon reinforced bags are the best but most expensive. They are made from ballistic nylon with a bubble wrap core. They come in either single or double sizes and have heavy zip closures. Some also have a separate wetsuit compartment.

A board bag may not seem essential to start with but to protect the trade-in value of your board it is well worth considering.

OTHER USEFUL ACCESSORIES

Most accessories are one-off purchases, apart from wax which has an annoying habit of melting all over the parcel shelf of the car or in the pocket of your jeans when left in the sun. An alternative to wax is a non-slip material that is stuck to the deck of the board, such as astro-deck. It is sold in kits designed to cover key grip areas on the deck such as the tail and back half of the board. The advantage of this traction-assisting material is that it stays clean and its adhesion under foot is constant, unlike wax that can come off or wear to a slippery polish half way through a surf session.

I mentioned rail savers earlier, again these are inexpensive items. If a leash is not attached to a rail saver the leash can in extreme cases chop the tail off a board like cheesewire. It is not cheap to have a board repaired and it takes time, usually when the surf is pumping.

If your board is fitted with one or more fin boxes, then one always seems to be missing – the screw and plate that holds the fin in place. These shake or vibrate themselves loose and disappear, or other surfers steal them. No matter how you lose them there is nothing more annoying than pulling on your cold wetsuit, getting your board out of its bag and finding the screw and plate missing. I place this device high on my list of accessories to carry with me constantly.

While on the subject of irritating things that can ruin a day at the beach, there is nothing more infuriating than driving to the beach and hearing a loud twang. Instinctively checking the rear vision mirror you see your surfboard bouncing down the road, or hanging out of the following car's windscreen. Roof racks and straps are more useful accessories that cost a fraction of a new surfboard, but most surfers put them at the bottom of their list of surfing essentials. Racks come in a variety of designs, from soft racks made of webbing and neoprene padded tubes, to hard racks that bolt on the gutters of the car roof.

For the transportation of a single board, soft racks are fine. They also stow away easily in the boot and if you go on a surfing holiday they fit into a board bag and can be quickly attached to a hire car. If your car is the communal surf bus and you transport the whole crew to the beach, invest in a set of hard racks. Preferably with a piece of high-tensile heavy gauge wire and a lock. A device is available that screws into the fin box and the wire can be passed through it and locked to the roof rack. In certain countries stealing surfboards is a business.

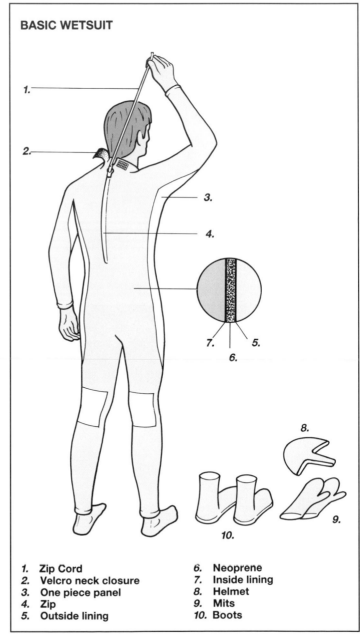

BASIC WETSUIT

1.	**Zip Cord**
2.	**Velcro neck closure**
3.	**One piece panel**
4.	**Zip**
5.	**Outside lining**
6.	**Neoprene**
7.	**Inside lining**
8.	**Helmet**
9.	**Mits**
10.	**Boots**

WETSUITS

Having detailed the accessories for surfboards a wet suit is high on my list of essentials. Like boards, wet-suits come in all shapes, colours and sizes. To confuse matters even further, they come in different thick-nesses. The suit is a thermal barrier between the body and the elements of wind and water. The suit, once wet, will soak up an amount of water which the body warms. This heat is stored in the hundreds of tiny cells in the layer of neoprene. Every time a surfer wipes out he gets a slight intake of fresh water and that is when you notice just how warm a wetsuit really does keep you. Wet-suits are tailored to fit standard sizes and can be bought off-the-peg or, as with boards, they can be custom-made. A wetsuit will last for many years if correctly looked after.

There are different neoprene thicknesses for different weather zones, and for winter and summer conditions. Please do not make the classic mistake and buy the thickest suit you can find thinking it will keep you much warmer. The few degrees it may add to your comfort will be lost in mobility. A thick wetsuit will restrict your movement and make it harder to paddle.

If you only want to surf in the sum-mer, then a thinner suit such as a 3/2mm combination will be adequate. If you intend to go surfing all year round then you will require a heavier thickness of neoprene such as a 4/3mm combination. Look for basic things such as a back zip with inside flap to stop leakage. More zips equal more trouble; ankle zips are prone to breaking, so avoid them. Knee reinforcement is vital for a beginner who will spend the first months learning to stand from a kneeling position. The seams are important, some suits are mouser stitched and leak slightly, other suits are blind stitched and glued and are totally watertight. The only water entry from a well-fitting suit should

Left: Wetsuit fit is very important. Too baggy and it will fill with water; too tight and the seams and stitching may split.

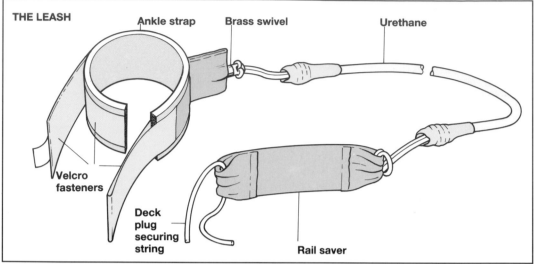

THE LEASH

Ankle strap   Brass swivel   Urethane

Velcro fasteners

Deck plug securing string

Rail saver

be from the natural absorption of the neoprene and may be very slightly through the neck and zip areas. If your location is very cold then a set of boots and gloves would be a good investment.

Getting into a wetsuit for the first time feels strange. When purchasing a wetsuit from a shop always try it on. Make sure the underarm panels fit well without bunching-up inside the suit. This will cause agonising wetsuit chafing in the armpit that in my experience seems to last for months and get worse with every surf session. Make sure the suit is long enough from the crotch to the neck without restricting bending.

Recently, surfers have started to wear brightly-coloured lycra vests to prevent rubbing. These vests or skins can be worn on their own to take away the wind chill or to protect a surfer from the sun's burning rays.

Spending long periods exposed to the burning sun not only gives surfers healthy tans, it increases the risk of skin cancer and eye problems. Specially-developed zinc-based creams are now widely used by surfers to protect your face from harmful rays. Sunglasses that block out 100% of the sun's infra-red and ultra-violet rays have been developed to protect the eyes while you are out there on the beach.

CHOOSING A SURFBOARD

Custom-built surfboards
These are the best buy. Always consult the shaper or surfshop manager. Give him full details of your skill or lack of it, he can then build or have built for you a surfboard that fits your requirements exactly. It is worth noting when choosing a custom board to find out the trade-in position with the company you are buying from. Always go to an established company; stay well clear of cheap backyard operations. They use sub-standard materials and offer no guarantee.

Moulded surfboards
If you took my advice and hired a surfboard to first try out surfing, it would

most probably have been a moulded one. Surfshops have a fleet of different shapes and lengths. Ask if you can have a hire-buy deal. You can first hire a few different boards and buy a new version of the one you like.

Secondhand boards
There are good deals to be found if you look hard enough. Always purchase from a reputable surf shop. Try to get a guarantee if possible; failing that ask them if you can try the board, leaving a deposit or full cash value. Once again find out what the position is when you want to trade the board in. If you buy privately you are unfortunately stuck with what you buy.

Left: A surfboard leash is probably the best surfing accessory ever invented. This inexpensive item eliminates the need to swim and retrieve your board, and acts as a life-saver, attaching you to your board in an emergency.

Right: Always put your leash on at the water's edge. Do not let it come into contact with sharp objects that might cut the elastic material, or the leash may snap when under tension.

Below: When waxing up your board, apply a thin layer of wax before each session. Here, particular attention is being paid to the new coat of wax, which is very important before surfing.

CHAPTER 3

BEGINNING TO SURF

If you are serious about learning to surf and have followed my advice by trying out the sport with an instructor, or even with a competent surfer, you will have experienced first-hand just how unstable a surfboard is in breaking surf. Most beginners find it difficult just to lie on the deck of a board without slipping off the side while they are bobbing around in the white-water.

To help familiarise yourself with the feel of a surfboard I suggest that you use dry land simulation. You may think you are going to look pretty silly pretending to surf on the beach but in my opinion it gives a beginner the feel of a surfboard beneath his or her body that will be invaluable when performing manoeuvres for the first time in the surf. Incidentally, windsurfers use dry land simulation to practise their manoeuvres with great effect, so do not dismiss dry land surfing simulation as being a waste of time.

When you can get from the prone paddling position to a fully standing surfing stance in one movement on dry land, it is time to slip into your shorts or wetsuit, wax up your board, and go surfing. One point to remember here: when putting on the leash, do not attach it to your ankle until you are about to enter the water. If you walk down to the beach with your leash on and the board under your arm you run the risk of either tripping over it or catching it on a rock or some other protruding object. Not only will you probably fall flat on your face, which is quite embarrassing, but also the nose of your board will almost certainly get damaged as it comes into contact with the beach.

Attach your leash to your back foot at the water's edge. This is where dry land simulation will have helped you. When you have practised getting from the prone paddling position to a standing position on the beach, you will have already chosen your stance and found out whether it is **natural** or **goofy** (see chapter 4) so you will know which foot points to the nose and which is the trailing or back foot on the tail. If you do not establish which foot is the rear foot before you enter the water, and you wrongly attach the leash to your front foot, you will either trip over it or the leash may wrap around your back foot when paddling making you wipe-out when you try to stand up.

Remember rule number one about beach safety – red flag, no surfing. Don't go charging into the surf fired with enthusiasm without first making sure that you are in the surfing area.

When you have managed to wade out through the first few lines of white-water to about waist depth, stop between waves, turn the board around, and when the next wave is approximately one metre from you push off the bottom with your feet, and then slide onto the board in the prone position.

Now you can enjoy the thrill of the wave carrying you in to the beach for the first time.

Below: Place the board on the beach, lay on the board making sure your feet are not overhanging the tail.

Below: In one continuous movement with your hand on the rail press down on the deck and lock your arms out straight.

DRY LAND SIMULATION

Choose a flat area of soft sand, making sure before you put the board down that there are no rocks or sharp objects underneath. Remove the fin from the box; if the fin is fixed then dig a hole in the sand to accommodate it. The natural rocker, or curve, of the board will cause a see-sawing effect. To stop this, pack some loose sand under the nose and tail. This also prevents the board from being subjected to any unnecessary stress.

Prone position

To establish approximately the prone position, lie on the board and put your toes on the tip of the tail. Do not let your feet hang over the tail. Once you are actually in the water you can adjust to the correct prone paddling position on your particular board. On your first session the waves you surf will be with you in this prone position. With your hands gripping the rails, this is fairly simple to do, very much like riding a big belly board.

Kneeling position

From the prone position grip the rails with both hands and in one movement move from the prone position to the kneeling stance. This is best achieved by keeping both hands parallel, and extending your arms into a press-up position. Once fully extended, slide your feet together under your body into a kneeling stance.

Once in this position do not stay upright but sit back on your lower legs and feet. Slide your hands back towards your body so that they are just in front of your knees. Once you are on a wave in this position you will be able to guide the surfboard by leaning to the left or right while still gripping the rails of the board.

Standing up

Getting to a kneeling position on a surfboard, especially on dry land, is quite easy. Even when you get into the surf it is quickly accomplished because a surfer has a lot of body contact with the board. Any instability can quickly be countered through body or hand pressure on the opposite side of the board.

In dry land manoeuvres it is very important to practise moving swiftly from position to position.

Moving from a prone position to a standing stance

Establish the approximate prone paddling flotation point by placing your toes on the tip of the tail and with both hands gripping the rails, push down and extend your arms in a press-up. Once your arms are locked out straight, slide your legs through under your body. At this stage you can either go into a kneeling position or go straight into a standing position. Technically, on the grounds of style, some surfers consider it wrong to move from the knees to a standing position, but many beginners simply cannot go straight into a standing stance.

Below: With your arms locked straight slide your feet through under your body bringing your front foot under your chest.

Below: With your front foot push down on the board and release your hand from the rails and stand up into a surfing stance.

Many surfers later find it hard to avoid the kneeling position when getting to their feet. When I explain these manoeuvres in the water later on in the chapter, I will look at this problem in more detail.

It is important to adopt the correct standing stance even at this stage. The stringer, the strip of wood that runs down the length of the board, is a guide to where your feet should be. Your front foot should be at a 90° angle to the stringer with your toes over one side and your heel over the other. Your back foot should also be in this position with your legs slightly bent and your feet approximately 24 inches (50 centimetres) apart.

Do not adopt a ski-type parallel stance with both feet either side of the stringer. Practise the dry land simulation until you can spring from a prone paddling position into a fully balanced surfing stance in one flowing movement. Dry land simulations such as this are sound basic first steps and when you feel happy with them go into the water.

SURF CONDITIONS

The best surf conditions occur when the wind blows offshore, that is, off the land onto the sea. Onshore wind blows from the sea onto the land and although the wind may be light and only chops up the surface, the waves can still be surfed. A strong-to-gale force onshore wind creates conditions that can still be surfed but the waves are lumpy and break in no set pattern. The beginner who will be spending his first sessions in the white-water will quickly need to learn how to read surf conditions. For instance, the first thing he or she will notice is that waves come in a series, known as **sets**, usually consisting of three waves with calm spells or "lulls" in between.

Rips and dangerous currents
When a wave breaks it discharges its energy and the water is pushed up the beach. The water then has to drain back down the beach. Let me illustrate this. If you take a bucket full of water and throw it up a 30° incline that is even, the water will run back down in a uniform pattern. If the incline has high and low points,

STAYING SAFE IN THE SURF

Red circle
The rip running back out to sea is extremely deceptive. Do not enter the water here; for a novice the rip is hard or impossible to paddle against.

Green circle
Always enter the water where the waves are breaking constantly. You may see expert surfers using the rip to get out. Never attempt to do so yourself

or mountains and valleys, then the water will drain off the high points and run into the low points, or channels. This is exactly what happens on the beach. Due to storm or wave action the top layer of sand constantly moves, forming high and low spots on the surface of the beach. The high spots are the **banks** that cause waves to break and peel left or right into the low spots called **rips**. These rip channels run back out to sea and because they are deeper than the banks they act like a river carrying the retreating water back into the surf. Experienced surfers use these rips to get out

Below: Beginners should never enter the water where a rip is running out to sea. Always ride the white-water waves, entering the water where they break.

beyond the surf. However, for beginners rips are dangerous because they run back out to sea at a much quicker rate than a beginner can paddle against.

A rip needs to be identified from the beach. You will notice that the incoming waves breaking in the rip break in a full and feeble manner. On a patrolled beach lifeguards set up the bathing area well away from these rip channels for obvious reasons. Sometimes however, in order to assist surfers paddling out or just because there is a lack of room on the beach, the rip may be on the edge of the surfing area. An inexperienced surfer should only

enter the water well away from the rip, in an area where the surf is breaking constantly.

If you get into the rip don't panic and try to paddle against it because you will use up too much energy. If you panic and lose your board swimming against the current is even harder than paddling. Instead, point your board out to sea and paddle along with the rip towards the breaking surf. Once the rip starts to find deeper water it loses strength and you will be able to paddle out of it into the breaking surf. From here you will be able to prone back to the beach, or signal for help from the lifeguards if necessary. Being

attached to your surfboard means that you have a flotation aid. I must stress that you should only use this course of action if you inadvertently get caught in the rip by moving tide or surf conditions. Do not ever jump into the rip instead of paddling out.

If you get really afraid in this situation, shout out to the nearest surfer for his or her assistance and ask them to signal for the lifeguard to assist you back to the beach. Always get out well beyond the breaking surf and do not attempt to paddle back to the beach without assistance. You may get caught by a breaking set of waves and lose your board which may put you in even greater danger.

ENTERING THE WATER

Take your board to the edge of the water in the surfing area and put on your leash. Before wading out with your board choose a spot that has constant breaking white-water waves. Stand either on the left or the right side of your board and point the nose out to sea. Never hold your board sideways on to the breaking waves. If a wave catches your board side-on this way the rail will hit you in the chest or face, or it will be pulled from your grip and possibly hit someone else standing or paddling out behind you. It is your responsibility to hold on to your board and keep control of it at all times. Beginners frequently get into a situation where the size of the incoming wave causes them to panic. Just because you are attached to your board by a leash and you know it will come back do not throw the board away and dive for the seabed to avoid the wave. A loose board in a crowded surfing area will almost certainly cause another surfer distress. Hang on to your board at all times. Eventually, you will learn how to get through waves either by rolling under them in an eskimo roll, or alternatively by sinking the board with your bodyweight.

When you have waded out to a waist-to-chest depth, turn the board around so that the nose faces the beach. Do this between sets to avoid getting the board side-on to the surf. Standing at the side of the

Below: Stand by your board and wait until the wave is approximately one metre away. Push off the bottom with your feet and slide smoothly onto the deck.

Bottom: Once the wave picks you up make sure you are not too far forward on the board. This will cause the nose of the board to dig in to the water.

board, hands held on each rail, wait until the approaching broken wave is about a metre away and then push off the bottom with your feet. Once you have practised this a few times it will be enough to get the board moving forward and once the wave picks up the board with you on it you have technically caught the wave. For the first few waves, simply lie in the prone position and enjoy the feeling of being carried to the beach. When the novelty of proning to the beach begins to wear off, the hard work starts.

STANDING UP

Pushing off in the same manner as before, catch the wave. Now push up so that your arms are fully extended and then slide your feet underneath your body. Next, kneel on the deck holding onto the rails with both hands and let the wave carry you to the beach as you did during the dry land simulation.

Once this becomes a natural feeling to you, try steering the board by leaning into a slight turn either left or right. Even at this elementary stage it is important for you to have gained control of your board.

As I mentioned earlier, there are two ways of getting from the prone to the standing position. Most beginners find it much easier to accomplish the whole manoeuvre if it is broken into four stages: prone, kneeling, half-stance, and full stance, with each of these stages mastered in order.

Surfers who learn this way sometimes find it hard to accomplish the prone-to-standing stance in one graceful, stylish manoeuvre much later. Surfing is as much about grace and style as it is about rip and carve, so bear this in mind. As soon as you feel happy standing up in four stages, then practise it in one flowing action. The stylists of the sport are right; if a surfer has a clumsy style and stance his or her overall performance is ruined.

When kneeling, try letting your hands off the rails and sliding one foot onto the deck in a half-kneeling, half-standing position.

From your previous experience of learning the proning-in manoeuvre,

you should now be able to gauge the proper paddling point – not too far forward or too far back. The combination of prone paddling out and learning to get into a standing stance, along with all the unsuccessful attempts that result in wipeouts, are great fun. Beginners now start to find muscles they were previously unaware they had!

You are now at the stage where you can paddle out to the first set of white-water, turn around, push off the bottom or paddle to catch the wave and prone in on the board, get to one knee without holding the rails and stand up, hopefully not wiping out too many times.

All this has been accomplished in the relative safety of the white-water without getting in the way of other more proficient surfers. The small white-water waves are fine for the purpose of learning the rudiments of the sport, but once accomplished it is time to venture a little further out to sea. This is a big step for the beginner. From this point you will be spending most of your time in water too deep to touch the bottom. Because you cannot now push off from the bottom you will have to learn to paddle the surfboard correctly to catch waves.

Once the security of being able to

Above: Push down with your arms, lock them out straight in a press up type action, slide your legs under the body and ride the wave to the beach.

stand up when anything goes wrong is taken away, you become more dependent on your surfboard for flotation and support – back to the platform theory. The only way to learn to paddle and sit on a surfboard is by practise. You may have felt a little silly doing those practise manoeuvres on dry land when learning to get on to one knee, but this is where technique comes into its own. Also, when there is surf you will be out there and able to pick up waves, but on flat days when there is no swell around you can take out your board and quite simply go for a paddle. This will build up your arm and back muscles and your stamina. On those hot summer days it is a great way to cool off, especially with a few of your friends. You can paddle around the headlands and coves; this is all part of the fun of learning the sport. The more time you spend in the water with your surfboard the better waterman you will become.

It is important at this stage to

Top left: Too far back on the board and it will paddle slowly.

Top right: Too far forward and the nose will go underwater to sink the board.

Above: The correct prone paddling position where the board travels quickly.

begin to build up knowledge of the sea and how it works, how to look after yourself, and how to be safe in it. As you progress, you will become aware of the different sea states. In the beginning it did not matter too much if the white-water you were riding was generated from offshore or onshore wind conditions, but now this is important.

WIND CONDITIONS

Now that you are getting to grips with the basics, you will start to notice just how important the wind direction really is. As I mentioned before offshore winds blow from the land onto the ocean and hold up the incoming waves, giving them clean rideable faces. Onshore wind blow-

Above: Find the correct point of balance and when the wave is approximately two metres away start to paddle. Make sure the wave has picked you up.

Above: Once the wave is caught and you can feel that it is pushing you and your board forward grip the rails and carefully start to push up.

Above: Pushing your body upwards in a press-up, lock out your arms and slide your legs under your body with your front foot under your chest.

Above: Clean entry into the water with your hands cupped is essential for good paddling.

storm generates impulses outward from the centre, which are ground swells. It has been estimated that a thirty foot swell would travel 3½ times around the world if a land mass was not in its way. It is the presence of a land mass that stops ground swell from an endless global journey. The Continental Shelf stretching out from the land under the sea, takes the full force of the incoming swell. Once the swell has travelled up the Shelf far enough to a point where it becomes too shallow to hold the size of the swell, the wave forms and breaks. A swell carries no water with it. It is an impulse moving through the water that will discharge its power when the wave breaks. The sea bed contour causes waves to have different characteristics. The beach break is generally more mellow than a reef break because it breaks on a sandy bottom. Reefs protrude upward from the sea bed making the swell break over the shallowest point of the reef. The bottom is hard rock or coral and is unforgiving, causing cuts, abrasions, and dings when a surfer wipes out. For the beginner, paddling out to a fast-breaking reef would be highly dangerous. Beach breaks on the other hand, with some exceptions, tend to break less aggressively in a slower manner – the bottom being sand – and are more forgiving on body and board.

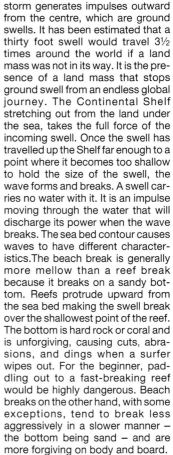

ing from the sea onto the land, blowing the waves over from behind, causes a choppy sea condition that is difficult to surf. The wind can blow from any direction, the best wind directions are offshore and side shore winds.

Onshore winds, if they blow strongly enough, can generate a wind swell. This is perfectly rideable but has less power than a ground swell. Cyclonic or low pressure areas far out at sea create storms and the wind disturbance on the ocean surface at the centre of the

Above: With your front foot in position release your grip on the rails at this point and rebalance your body before attempting to stand up on the board.

Above: With your back leg push upwards, leaning slightly forward. Rebalance your body, bringing your centre of gravity upwards from the board.

Above: Assume a full standing stance with your feet across the stringer and your knees slightly bent. Use your upper body movement to maintain balance.

CHAPTER 4

SURFING UNBROKEN WAVES

So far I have explained the very basic techniques of learning to handle a surfboard in white-water by logical step-by-step progression. When you take up surfing you will find that a lot of the basic manoeuvres fall into place simultaneously, so you do not have to become accomplished in one step before tackling the next. For instance, if you start to surf at the beginning of summer and you live in a location that has good, constant surfing conditions, taking up a new pastime will naturally fire your enthusiasm and you will be spending as much time at the beach in the waves as possible. So with this constant practise you can expect to make quick progress, simultaneously learning and perfecting a lot of the basics. In fact, by the end of the summer you could well be surfing to a competent standard.

As I have mentioned in chapter 2, the dry land simulation technique will have given you an awareness of the basics before you get down seriously to learning to surf. Often, people take up the sport with a friend or friends which is a bonus because an element of competition is introduced to see who can stand and surf before anyone else! There will also be a thread of humorous criticism running through the group

about style and technique, or the lack of both. This all adds to the fun of spending hot summer days at the beach as you make progress.

SMALL SURF

The next stage to master is in small surf when the white-water is minimal, and a surfer can easily paddle out to the **line-up**. When it is small everyone will be trying to catch any waves that are breaking so you will be amongst proficient surfers. It is not a case of one moment you are a bather armed with a surfboard learning to ride broken white-water waves, and the next you are a competent surfer. Surfing ability relies on constant, gradual improvement punctuated with periodic leaps forward in skill. For instance, the first time you try to stand up you will probably fall off. When you start standing and keeping your balance on nine out of ten waves, you have accomplished a major step. So when you paddle out in small surf into the line-up and catch your first proper peeling wave, the process starts again; when you can catch and ride a large proportion of these outside waves with some degree of control, you have reached another major step.

Once you have sampled the thrill

of dropping down the face of your first real wave, you will never again be satisfied with riding white-water waves. You must now learn the technique of getting out through the white-water to these line-up waves and catching them. To start with you may have been amongst experienced surfers in the line-up on small surf days and taken note of how they select and catch waves, then tried for yourself and found one of two things. Either the wave passed you by no matter how hard you paddled, or the wave picked you up and slammed you and your board nose first onto the bottom.

First, we should look at some paddling techniques, how to paddle out, selecting and catching waves, the take-off area, who has the right of way and what to do in an emergency. Because a lot of these techniques are learnt simultaneously, I will then progress to wave-riding techniques such as dropping into waves, angling the take-off, riding the wall of the waves, trimming the surfboard, and kicking off the wave. You are now venturing into deeper, more dangerous water. Never attempt to surf in waves that are too big; use the experience you have already gained to judge the size of the surf. Remember how important it is never to take risks.

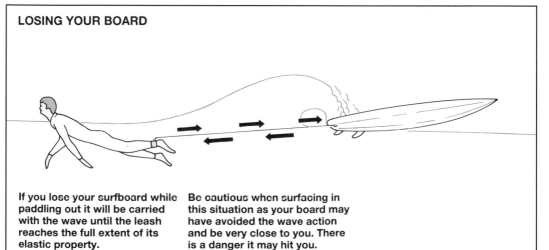

LOSING YOUR BOARD

If you lose your surfboard while paddling out it will be carried with the wave until the leash reaches the full extent of its elastic property.

Be cautious when surfacing in this situation as your board may have avoided the wave action and be very close to you. There is a danger it may hit you.

PADDLING OUT

To start with, let me remind you once again of the safety rules. No. 1 – Red Flag, No. 2 – Surfing Area. Now a new rule has to be observed – courtesy and conduct to other surfers. You are attempting to get out through breaking surf to a given point where surfers take off on the outside waves. This requires a certain amount of stamina and skill. Other surfers will now be in close proximity to you. Be aware of the surfers around you. Look behind you, make sure when you paddle out that the wave is not going to push you back into another surfer. Do not throw your board away in a crowded surfing area. Many beginners think that discharging their surfboard and diving under waves is easier than trying to push through a wave. I have seen too many accidents caused by surfers indiscriminately throwing away their board to avoid a possible battering by a breaking wave. It is not good policy to throw away your board for your own personal safety. If the wave catches the board it may not be washed away from you, so you are then faced with the prospect of being hit by your own board so be aware of other surfers and do not endanger them or yourself by your actions.

The correct technique of paddling out is best described in a number of phases: Wait for a lull in the intensity or frequency of the waves, always paddle out in the calm spells between sets to conserve your energy. Pick a point where you want to end up. This will usually be the take-off area where surfers are catching waves. Paddle out making sure that no-one is paddling behind or in front of you. If the waves are breaking in peaks, paddle diagonally between them to avoid getting caught by a wave. Quite often whilst paddling out a surfer will get caught by a

Right: Always paddle out in a lull between sets of waves.

DEALING WITH A BREAKING WAVE

If you get caught by a breaking wave try to push through it by sinking your board. Either push it under the wave with your bodyweight or get off and sink the nose and keep a tight grip. Never throw away your board to avoid the wave action.

wave which will push them quite a way backwards. There are various techniques to avoid or lessen the amount of ground lost, but at this level of proficiency there is very little a beginner can do once caught in this position. If the wave has broken and is rolling towards you there are two methods to lessen the amount of distance the wave will carry you backwards. First, slide your body up to the nose and sink the board, wrapping your legs under the rails and gripping the board as tightly as possible. This has the effect of sinking the nose so that the wave cannot push water underneath the board. It will not get you through every wave nor will it stop the heavy wave action you will encounter, but it will lessen the distance the wave will push you

Below: Paddle up the face to the top of the wave and before the lip strikes, sink your board to tuck it through the back.

Below: If the wave has broken, sink the board under the white-water as far as possible by pushing down on the nose.

DISCARDING YOUR BOARD

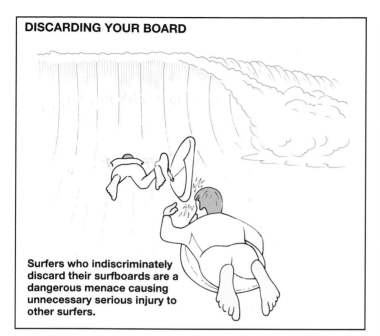

Surfers who indiscriminately discard their surfboards are a dangerous menace causing unnecessary serious injury to other surfers.

backwards. The second method is not often used by modern-day surfers because it was really designed to get the old heavy 9 feet 6 inch (3 metre) board rider out of trouble – the "Eskimo Roll". When a wave breaks in front of you or on top of you, grip the rails in the same manner as you would if you were catching a wave and getting to your feet, then roll off the board turning it

over at the same time. This sinks the board with your body weight hanging underneath it. The amount of board area the wave comes into contact with is far less.

Close-out sets or sneaker waves

If we consider a typical paddle-out situation that goes wrong and you get caught inside. You are paddling

out between sets and what is known as a **sneaker,** or **close-out set** breaks further out than the normally set waves. It is going to clean everybody up; some worse than others. Your problem is that this wall of water is bigger than those you have previously encountered.

Along with the panic it is causing, you have to make a swift decision – how to deal with the situation. After paddling nearly all the way out you do not want to lose the valuable ground already gained, so the obvious answer is to have a go at getting through it by either sinking the nose of the board or doing an Eskimo roll.

If this is not possible then try slipping off the side of the board, grabbing the leash close to the board to stop it stretching, and sinking the board with your bodyweight. This stops the elastic action of the leash and the board and rider stay together. This emergency action has its dangers because the board and surfer are together and stand a chance of coming into contact. If you do not fancy your chances of getting through the wave, first make sure there is no-one behind you, if there is you have to hang on to your board and try to make it through the wave, or at least keep control by hanging on to the leash. If all is clear then turn the board around to face the beach. Get into a prone position and slide towards the back so that the nose is well out of the water. Doing this ensures that when the wave strikes it does not pick up the board and dig in the nose, causing the board and rider to cartwheel end over end.

Once the wave picks up the board, grip the rail firmly and prone in until the wave loses most of its power. You have lost valuable ground but at least you have not thrown away your board causing other surfers distress and danger. Every surfer develops his or her own technique of paddling out and this is very much a case of trial and error.

The major considerations at all times are the safety of other surfers in close proximity and your own personal safety. Never attempt to paddle out if you think there is an element of risk.

Above: Sitting comfortably on the board in the line-up waiting for the next set of waves to arrive.

Below: When you paddle for a wave always catch the wave on the peak. Keep an eye on the peak when taking off.

THE LINE-UP

When you get outside behind the breaking waves take a few minutes to familiarise yourself with your surroundings. Most surfers sit on their boards while watching the horizon for incoming waves. Once they have assessed where a wave is going to peak, they paddle over to catch it.

Now you have to learn to sit on the board and select waves and then learn how to catch them. This is managed by the following steps.

Sitting on your board

I will not make too much of this because it is mastered quite easily. The hardest part is getting from the paddling position to the sitting position. The easiest way is to slide back towards the tail, let the nose come up out of the water, allow your legs to go over the rails, and sit up. The same applies in reverse when you are in a paddling position ready to catch a wave.

Wave selection

The hardest part of selecting waves is learning how to read them. From the moment a wave begins to "feather" it can be caught. If you try to catch it too early the wave will pass underneath you and no amount of frantic paddling will help you catch the wave. If a wave is taken too late then the board and you will get pitched out with the lip of the breaking wave. This is quite unpleasant and is similar to going over a waterfall equivalent in size on a board. Hence the term "over the falls". Wave selection is the art of anticipating how and where the wave will break and later as you gain more knowledge of waves you will be able to anticipate how the wave will form and break all the way down the line or wall. It is going to take you time and several savage wipe-outs before you can catch waves easily. Next, you have to learn to get to your feet as quickly as possible in one flowing movement.

Catching waves and standing

At first the frustration of not being able to catch waves leads to surfers attempting to catch waves that are too "critical" or too far advanced in the process of breaking for them to handle. This makes it necessary to rethink the situation. You should try to follow the example of those surfing around you. Do not try to catch any wave; select a wave that is peaking, and paddle down the face. Once you feel the sensation of being carried forward then push down

with your arms until they are locked out straight, and slide your feet through under your body and stand up. At first you will find this action hard, if not impossible, to manage.

Again, think about it in stages. First catch the wave and prone down the face. Once into the trough of the wave it will break behind you,

then stand up. This should be repeated but try to stand up earlier each time you catch a wave. Eventually you will be able to catch the wave and take the drop straight down the face of the wave. Once you are capable of catching and surfing down the face of a wave another of those big steps I talked of earlier has been achieved. When you link this new manoeuvre with the white-water manoeuvres you have previously learnt, you can now take off and surf from the outside all the way into the beach.

A lot of the manoeuvres are learnt simultaneously. For example, a surfer, once he or she can take the drop down a wave, will start angling the board to the left or right.

From this point we are ready to move on to the next stage, which involves learning to surf across the face or wall of the wave using the correct part of the wave by angling the board on take-off to the left or right.

Left and right hand waves pose a problem for beginners. The two stances in surfing are **natural foot** and **goofy foot,** which both refer to the position of the front or leading foot. Putting the left foot forward means a surfer is natural-footed while a surfer putting his or her right foot forward is goofy-footed. The majority of surfers are natural-footed, and most of the world's famous waves are right-hand breaking. It is far easier to surf facing the wave (forehand) than having your back to it (backhand). Now, just to totally confuse you, a lot of surfers will stand up forehand on either a left or a right breaking wave. These are called switch-footed surfers. Fortunately this does not last long and once they have found which

Above left: Paddle with the wave until you feel it pick up the board and start to propel it forward. Look down the line of the wave in the direction you are travelling.

Left: Push the board down into the face and decide what form of turn to perform. This can either be a top angle or a bottom turn.

stance offers the most control they will become either natural or goofy accordingly.

When you become competent at catching waves and getting to your feet, you will probably only be able to go straight down the face of the wave with some degree of control. Once the wave has broken it starts to churn around under the board, making control difficult and quite often this will end in a wipe-out. The object of surfing is not to travel straight in with the wave, but to surf the face or wall of the breaking wave.

Having established that you are a goofy or natural foot, you will find it much easier to travel forehand along a wave.

THE RULES

Once you have practised the basics of paddling and balance and can with some degree of accuracy catch waves and control your surfboard you will be paddling out, catching waves back to the beach, and paddling out again, all of which will be done in close proximity to others. Surfing does not yet have an official rule book but there is a code of conduct that you as a beginner will have to learn. Failure to observe these few laws of common courtesy will inevitably end in you being put clearly in the picture by those you have impeded.

Who has the right of way on a wave?

The right of way indisputably belongs to the surfer who is nearest to the peak, or pocket, of the wave. To drop in on this surfer puts them in a potentially dangerous position because the path they would have taken along the wave has been blocked by the surfer who has dropped in, forcing the surfer with the right of way to change their planned route along the wave and this may lead to an unnecessary wipe-out.

Above: The surfer on the left has been dropped in on as he turns off bottom. The offending surfer is directly in his way.

Beginners who are unaware of the right of way always treat a wave with the attitude that it is theirs, even if someone else is on it. This is the biggest cause of accidents. Imagine the case of a surfer with the right of way taking off in a critically steep part of the wave. All the other experienced surfers who were pad-

THE DROP-IN RULE

The right of way on a wave lies with the surfer (in green) who is nearest to the peak. Never drop in on him. If you both catch the wave kick off immediately giving him the right of way.

Above: Never abandon your board. The surfer on the wave is in such a critical position he cannot avoid a serious collision.

dling for that wave pull off and the surfer with the right of way lines up the wall of the wave to start performing manoeuvres. Suddenly, the path is blocked by a beginner attempting to take off making a collision inevitable. If you blatantly drop in on someone, be prepared for the worst – a bad gash in your body or board.

What to do when paddling out if a big wave either breaks on top of you or in front of you

First check there is nobody paddling out behind you, if there is do not throw away your surfboard and dive for security under the breaking wave with the confidence that once the wave has passed over you your board will return by the leash.

If there are no other surfers in close proximity and the wave approaching you is going to cause you serious distress, and in your judgement ditching your board will lessen the hammering the wave will give you, then, and only then, discharge your board. Later in the book I will tell you how to **duck dive** and then apart from exceptional cases there will be no need to throw away your board in panic. It is a much better policy to keep your board under your control than throw it away. Imagine the amount of accidents that could happen if every surfer adopted the attitude that it is easier to throw the board away than try to push through the wave.

If you are on a wave and lose control of your surfboard in a crowded area, what do you do?

Do not simply bail out and let your board go. The leash is there for a reason – to stop the board getting washed all the way to the beach, causing mayhem in a crowded area along the way. If you lose control and fall off, make an attempt to grab the leash as near to the board as possible. This will stop the leash stretching too far and will keep the board near you. Remember, the wave you take off on is for your pleasure. If you foul it up it is still your wave and your problem. Too many novices flop off their boards into the water and let their boards go, causing others distress and injury.

What to do if you are in a situation where a collision is inevitable

Again if you are paddling out and a collision is on the cards, do not let go of your board. Either flip it over like an Eskimo roll or slip off the opposing side of impact and sink your board and body as deep as possible. The principle is to mini-mise your vulnerable body area exposed to the oncoming surfer allowing him as much space as possible to turn away and avoid impact. It is much better for his fin to strike your board than your body. If you are in the reverse position and find another surfer in your path and a collision is a possibility, slow your board down as much as possible by pushing down on the tail with your back foot and digging it into the wave. This will act as a brake and slow you down. At the same time try to straighten out towards the beach to avoid the impact; never jump off and let the other surfer take all the impact whilst you dive under the water to protect yourself.

Right: Boogie boarders are particularly vulnerable because their boards are shorter than surfboards. They trail their legs and feet behind them and also they do not seem to understand the drop-in rule and quite often get run over.

CHAPTER 5

BASIC SURFING DISCIPLINES

Remember the stable platform theory I mentioned in previous chapters. The beginner's board, being more stable than a more refined shorter surfboard, is ideal for learning the next set of manoeuvres. Because it is wider, longer and thicker, a surfer can catch waves much easier and earlier than if he or she was riding a shorter, less buoyant surfboard. I mention this because a beginner's board will by now have been well used and starting to show signs of all those wipe-outs when it came into contact with others, or on those occasions when the leash snapped and the board went straight up on to the sand hitting the only rock on the entire beach.

So with your faithful old platform looking none too good there is a great temptation to change or trade-in your board for something a little racier – my advice is don't do this until it is absolutely necessary.

Stick with your beginner's board until you have mastered the following five manoeuvres.

Angle take-off

Angling the board in the same direction as the wave is breaking. From this take-off you can put the surfboard into a good trim position without bottom-turning.

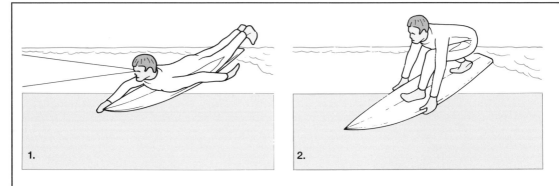

FOREHAND ANGLE TAKE-OFF

1. Paddling at the same angle as the wave is about to break, look down the line of the wave, paddle with the wave until it starts to carry you and your board with it.

2. Once the board starts to gain forward momentum, powered by the wave, push down on the rails and slide to a standing surfing stance in one flowing movement.

BACKHAND ANGLE TAKE-OFF

1. As with the forehand manoeuvre, paddle and catch the wave. The angle should be slightly tighter to the wave. Sight down the wave. It is much more difficult to accomplish this with your back to the breaking wave.

2. Once forward momentum under the wave power is achieved, slide up into a surfing stance, slightly dropping at the

Left: Angle the board in the direction the wave will break, paddle, and catch the wave. When the wave picks up the board, line up the wave.

Right: Push the board down into the wave and as the wave steepens behind, push up with your arms until they are out straight. Then stand up and turn in one easy movement.

3.

4.

3. Once into a full standing stance with your lower body slightly compressed and knees bent, sight down the line of the wave and turn into trim.
4. Coming out of the angle turn into the trim position. This will accelerate your board because it is travelling in the optimum power band of the wave. The manoeuvre is now complete and the board is in perfect trim.

3.

4.

same angle, and bring your body into a full surfing stance.
3. Sight down the line and prepare to adjust the dropping angle to place the board into a full trim position. Remember to constantly watch the wave.
4. Coming out of the turn adjust the board into the trim position of the wave. When you angle take-off avoid riding only easy forehand waves.

Bottom turn

That is, taking off at a straighter angle than the angle take-off, dropping down the wave and turning off the bottom of the wave. All this should be done in a flowing sequence.

Cutback

Once on the wall of the wave, through an angled take-off or bottom turn, and in a good trim position, a surfer will outrun the wave, ending up out on the shoulder. To get back to the power pocket of the wave, a cutback must be performed

from the shoulder back along the wave into the pocket. This manoeuvre involves elements of backhand and forehand surfing.

Left: This surfer has dropped in and turned using the angle take-off. Note his back foot putting pressure on the inside rail.

Right: Dropping in along the wave at a complementary angle to the direction of the breaking wave, he will now place his board up into the wave.

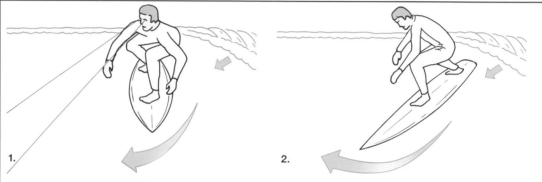

1. 2.

FOREHAND BOTTOM TURN

1.   Paddle and catch the wave and then slide up into a standing stance in one flowing move. Point the board down at the base of the wave. Compress your body and legs.
2.   Once you have dropped to the bottom gaining speed, push down on the inside rail and adjust the direction of the board slightly before performing the turn.
3.   The board is now ready to turn so push down hard on the inside rail and dig the tail into

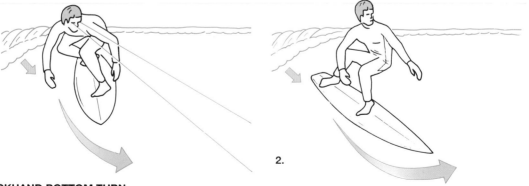

1. 2.

BACKHAND BOTTOM TURN

1.   Slightly more difficult to perform than the forehand version, the surfer having his back to the wave and therefore there is a "blind spot" when executing the manoeuvre. Again the same applies as with the forehand turn, paddle and catch the wave. I suggest you start by angling the board slightly in the direction the wave is breaking, sight down the line to assess where to turn.
2.   Placing pressure on the tail through the inside rail, slightly

Left: Once up on the wall and into the trim position note how he compresses his lower body to tackle breaking sections on the wave.

A basic off-the-lip, rollercoaster or re-entry

On the wall, in a trim position, a surfer may encounter sections of the wave that are breaking in front of him. He must either go around the section, through it, over it, or rebound off it. The action needed is to swing the board up to hit the lip or

3.

4.

the wave. With your front foot guide the board around and then sight an imaginary point to perform the next manoeuvre. Once the board is pointing back

up to the point of impact, release the inside rail pressure.
4. The board is now on a track up the face towards the lip. Place pressure on the outside

edge through the ball and heel of your foot and adjust the angle. The board can now either be rebounded off the lip or trimmed under the lip.

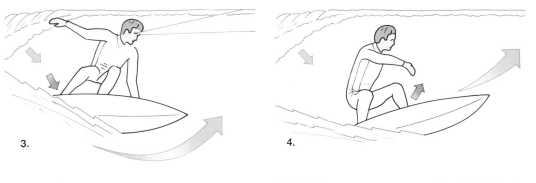

3.

4.

adjust the angle of the board before actually performing the manoeuvre. Drop with the wave to the chosen point.
3.   Here, push the board down

on the inside rail. Guide the board fully round.
4.   At this point look down the line to a point on the wave that will get you into a good trim slot

or rebounding off the lip. Once you are pointing towards the spot for your next manoeuvre pressure on the inside rail can be gradually released.

form at an imaginary impact point, then drop back down, turn off the bottom, and back into trim.

Climbing and dropping

In the trim position on the wall of the wave a surfer can perform a rail-to-rail transitional movement that causes the board to rise or fall at the wave face in order to accelerate the surfboard. The board is constantly rocking from one rail to the other. If you watch professional contest surfers, they constantly "pump" the board in this manner between manoeuvres to maintain a constant speed.

These five manoeuvres give you the basic disciplines of dropping in and surfing the wall of the wave. Running again quickly through the sequence:

□ You can either angle take off or bottom turn or a combination of both.

□ Once on the wall, to get back into a good trim position back in the pocket of the wave perform a cutback.

□ To get around the sections of breaking waves drop to the bottom of the wave and go around it, or go up the wave and rebound off it.

□ To keep the board flowing between manoeuvres use a climbing and dropping series of weight transfers from rail to rail. This will also keep the board responsive.

Technique here will be difficult to learn because most beginners are too stiff and stick-like when they are on a surfboard, so when they go into a bottom turn, for instance, they dig the inside rail and fall off. This set of new manoeuvres requires a flowing agility in order to perform them correctly. To help loosen up the body many surfers practise stretching exercises so that when they enter the water they are supple and relaxed.

Also, mental attitude has to be right. When a beginner starts these manoeuvres he or she will find them difficult to master. Some people may be inclined to lose interest at this stage if they cannot overcome this barrier. The key to mastering this next phase is having the right mental approach. In other words getting stuck in, paddling harder,

Right: Here, the surfer takes off preparing himself for the whole drop-in and turn manoeuvre.

Bottom right: Pushing the board into the wave he stands and instinctively judges how and what turn to use on the wave. Dropping to the bottom he releases his back foot pressure from the turn.

competing for waves, watching your peers, asking advice and most important of all, having dedication. When things seem to be going from bad to disastrous, do not paddle in and throw your board on the beach in despair. Try to analyse just what you are trying to accomplish. Break the manoeuvre down into basic steps, then take each step and critically look at how you are performing it. Each of the five basic manoeuvres of surfing are inter-related and they are accomplished by transferring the weight from one rail to the other. This is combined with a flowing movement that involves just about every part of the body. Many beginners tend to watch more experienced surfers and attempt to copy their "style". This results in all kinds of body gyrations and wiggles that have no functional use whatsoever. Keep your style simple; flow from one move to the next. As you gradually build on your repertoire of manoeuvres your style will improve.

The best way to assess your performance is by video. Get a friend to video you performing both forehand and backhand manoeuvres, then critically analyse what you are doing wrong. If you surf with one or more friends get together and take each other's performances apart with critical constructive criticism. Then go back in the water and try to build on what you have learnt. When I was learning to surf an experienced surfer who surfed our local beach regularly paddled over to me and told me what I was doing wrong. At first I resented his interference but he persisted and we eventually became friends. Under his supervision I successfully learnt the basic manoeuvres in half the time of my friends.

I mentioned earlier that your board may be showing signs of wear. There are two ways to fix a surfboard. The first is to take it to a surf shop or board factory and sit on the beach watching your friends surf, and wait, often for a long time, until they get round to fixing it. Secondly, do it yourself. Basic dings are quite easily fixed. After I have run through the five basic manoeuvres I will explain how to do this.

Let us assume that you can paddle and catch a wave, stand up and ride straight in with some degree of control. The next basic step to master is the angle take-off, both forehand and backhand. Before explaining this manoeuvre I would

Above right: Note the nose of the board; he is still keeping a certain amount of pressure on the tail. This has a stalling effect.

Right: Once the wave starts to hollow he releases the pressure and leans forward and is placed perfectly in the pocket of this peeling right hand wave.

just like to run through forehand and backhand surfing. Most surfers at this stage find it far easier to surf when they are facing the wave (forehand). On 99 percent of the waves they ride they will attempt to go forehand even if the wave is not breaking in that direction they will still take off and try to surf facing the wave. This can be quite drastic. Take for instance a wave breaking to the left and a surfer turns to the right and attempts to ride into the peak or straight up the tube the wrong way. He or she is going to get clobbered. If the wave is a right then surf right. If it is a left then go to the left. The only way to learn to go backhand is through constant practise. Elements of the backhand turn are part of a cutback manoeuvre so it is important to be equally competent on the forehand or backhand.

The following section of the book is written manoeuvre by manoeuvre in an effort to avoid confusion. I have put the following manoeuvres into a logical sequence but you do not have to strictly follow the order.

ANGLE TAKE-OFFS

First select the wave, and then paddle at the same angle the wave is about to break. It helps if it is breaking backhand to paddle at a more acute angle so that when the wave is caught and the surfer stands up he or she can get into trim.

When you have caught the wave get into a standing stance. Look down the wall of the wave aiming to trim your board about halfway up the wall. Push down on the inside rail with your back foot, and at the same time swing the board up the wave with your lower body while guiding the board with your front foot. Once you have hit the spot where you judged the trim position to be, release the pressure on the inside rail and straighten the board so the nose is pointing straight down the line of the wave. You

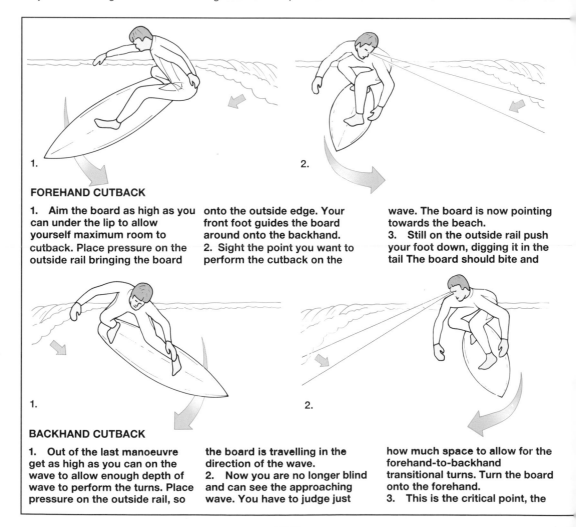

FOREHAND CUTBACK

1. Aim the board as high as you can under the lip to allow yourself maximum room to cutback. Place pressure on the outside rail bringing the board onto the outside edge. Your front foot guides the board around onto the backhand.
2. Sight the point you want to perform the cutback on the wave. The board is now pointing towards the beach.
3. Still on the outside rail push your foot down, digging it in the tail The board should bite and

BACKHAND CUTBACK

1. Out of the last manoeuvre get as high as you can on the wave to allow enough depth of wave to perform the turns. Place pressure on the outside rail, so the board is travelling in the direction of the wave.
2. Now you are no longer blind and can see the approaching wave. You have to judge just how much space to allow for the forehand-to-backhand transitional turns. Turn the board onto the forehand.
3. This is the critical point, the

should now be in trim.

Once you can angle take-off and trim your board, you will be able to put together the rest of the basic manoeuvres. Again, I must stress that these are not learnt one at a time, but simultaneously, by the time that you have mastered the angle take-off you will also be start-

Right: A surfer cutting back along the wave to the power pocket. Notice his back foot compressed pushing down hard on the inside rail, dropping his bodyweight into the backhand part of the cutback.

3.

4.

snap around onto the backhand. If you go too far you will meet the oncoming white-water, making the cutback more difficult. As you enter the critical

power pocket, transfer your weight to the inside rail.
4.   The board is turned back onto the forehand in a pivot-type turn, snapping the board around

on the tail in the hollow section in front of the pocket. Now you are back in the peak, or pocket, sighting down the line to the point of your next move.

3.

4.

board has to be quickly brought around onto the backhand. You are more vulnerable on your backhand to digging the outside rail.

4.   Having gained the maximum height before performing the change back into backhand mode. Release weight on the inside rail and transfer to the

outside rail. It needs to be done gently at first. Once the nose is around and there is no danger of catching the inside edge then the tail can be dug in.

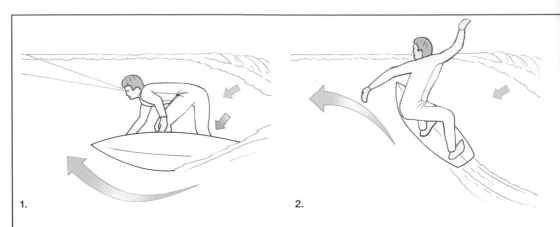

1.   2.

FOREHAND TOP TURN OR OFF THE LIP

1.   Place pressure on the inside rail, pushing it down into the wave face, guiding the board around and up the wave to a predetermined point of impact with the lip of the wave.
2.   Once the surfboard is on track up the wave to the point of impact you can decide whether to perform a turn under the lip or re-entry off the lip. Your weight is transferred to the outside rail.
3.   As you attack the manoeuvre push the tail in hard with your rear foot on the outside rail

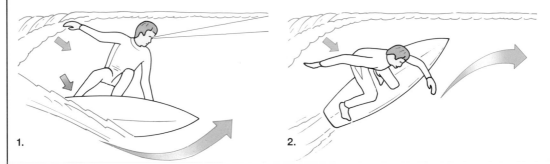

1.   2.

BACKHAND TOP TURN OR OFF THE LIP

1.   Again slightly more difficult than on forehand, press down on the inside rail. Drop the centre of your bodyweight, leaning slightly into the turn, your front foot will guide the board around. If you "overcook" this part of the manoeuvre, the board's inside rail will dig and the board will stop. Once on the inside rail pick your point of impact to execute your manoeuvre.
2.   The board is driven up the face from the speed generated from the bottom turn. You are

ing to learn to climb and drop in and out of trim, and how to cope with breaking sections along the wave.

You could perhaps quite happily angle take-off and cruise along the wall of the wave for the rest of your surfing career, and in fact some surfers do, but this is not what surfing is all about. You need to aim to get into the critical section of the waves in order to perform manoeuvres in the power pocket. The angle take-off can be supplemented with the angle bottom turn

to start with, and then eventually a full bottom turn.

You can drive the board hard off the bottom or base of the wave, turning the board back up into the trim position.

Alternatively, if the wave is sectioning, you can go straight up into the lip and turn using the power from the bottom, turning under the lip back down the face. Then, it is possible to bounce off the lip or whitewater back down the wave into another manoeuvre.

BOTTOM TURN

Using the angle take-off to begin with, point your board at a less acute angle to the wall of the wave and paddle to catch the wave instead of standing up. Push your board down the wave with your arms, slide to your feet while at the same time continue pointing your board towards the base of the wave. When the section of wave starts to feather in front of you, turn your board off the bottom of the wave.

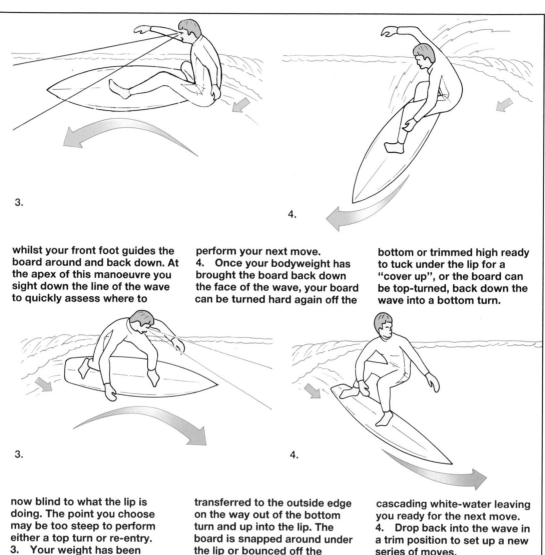

3.

4.

whilst your front foot guides the board around and back down. At the apex of this manoeuvre you sight down the line of the wave to quickly assess where to

perform your next move.
4.   Once your bodyweight has brought the board back down the face of the wave, your board can be turned hard again off the

bottom or trimmed high ready to tuck under the lip for a "cover up", or the board can be top-turned, back down the wave into a bottom turn.

3.

4.

now blind to what the lip is doing. The point you choose may be too steep to perform either a top turn or re-entry.
3.   Your weight has been

transferred to the outside edge on the way out of the bottom turn and up into the lip. The board is snapped around under the lip or bounced off the

cascading white-water leaving you ready for the next move.
4.   Drop back into the wave in a trim position to set up a new series of moves.

What you are in fact doing is delaying the moment you make the turn. Build up speed as the board drops down the face; this speed is released when the board is finally turned. Once you have successfully made a few angle take-off bottom turns then start to lessen the angle that the board is pointing in relation to the wave, and point it more towards the beach. Drop down the face and drive hard off the bottom by pushing down on the inside rail. If this is done too savagely then the

board will dig in and stop.
As the board comes off the bottom, look down the wave and pick an imaginary point of impact where you are going to attempt your next manoeuvre. If the peak you have selected to take off on is sectioning and about to break, you can revert back to the angle taken to first get into the wave. Then, once you have made it around the section, climb high on the wall and drop to the bottom, pushing your board off the inside rail. This combination of

angling the take-off, combined with a semi-bottom turn, works well and can be blended into one smooth manoeuvre.
There are several combinations that surfers use when taking off on a wave. You should be looking to achieve one flowing manoeuvre: standing up while dropping to the bottom with a combination of foot and body movements. Get your board on to the inside rail, releasing the outside rail from the water. With less area of surfboard in contact

with the wave it will turn or pivot around much more quickly. When your board has reached the full extent of the turn, the pressure on the inside rail is released to drop the outside rail back into the water. Now you are ready to perform your next manoeuvre.

Once you have accomplished a turn and have the board in a controlled trim position on the wave face, your board will accelerate as the wave breaks behind it. As the board speeds along the wall it outruns the breaking wave. If you wish you can keep going and kick off over the shoulder or cutback into the wave. The cutback is a series of 'S' turns that puts the surfer back into the power pocket of the wave.

CUTBACK

As the board speeds along the wall, you must pick a point to perform the cutback. The point where the manoeuvre is performed is critical if you start too early then you will get caught by the breaking wave in mid-manoeuvre. If it is performed too far out on the shoulder your board will bog down or catch a rail due to lack of speed. The first part of the cutback contains elements of both forehand and backhand surfing. When you first try to perform a cutback you may find it difficult to correctly time the backhand to forehand switch-over. So, the whole manoeuvre needs to be broken down into stages. To start with, the board has to be turned around in a manoeuvre that will put it on its outside rail. Your back foot is placed on the tail of the board; your body weight is split 60% on your back foot and 40% on your front foot. The outside rail is pushed into the wave and around in the opposite direction to the way you have been travelling. The first attempt will result in the board moving only a few degrees

Right: This surfer has outrun the wave and needs to place his board back along the wave to the centre of energy in the wave. To perform a cutback, the tail is pushed in and around hard on the inside rail.

out of the straight line in which it is travelling.

The technique employed to perform a cutback takes a combination of timing and anticipation. It has to be performed in a hollowish section of the wave because this allows the board to be put on to the rail and carried back around. Once the board has come around on the first part of the manoeuvre it has then got to be turned back in the opposite direction on the inside rail. Allow the board to drop back on to a flat plane while at the same time judging the approaching wave. Pressure must be applied to the outside rail to get the board back around and moving in the same direction as the approaching power pocket of the wave.

Once the cutback has been completed you need to get quickly into a trim position on the wave and anticipate the section of wave ahead to start your next manoeuvre. The whole idea is to keep as close to, or in, the critical part of the wave or pocket. As the wave breaks it will section along the wall. This means that parts of the top start to roll down the face. The wave may also close out down its entire length at this stage.

Unpredictable waves

Please note that I am describing ideal waves and how to perform ideal manoeuvres. In practice every wave is different and the manoeuvre may not be possible to perform because of its peculiar wave characteristics. For example, on beach breaks with shore break peaks, the waves tend to be short so you do not have a long wall to work on. You will need constantly to keep cutting back to stay in the critical part of the wave. Therefore it is difficult, if not impossible, on most of these types of waves to perform more than a basic set of manoeuvres, such as a turn, cutback and re-entry, before the wave closes out.

On a long-walling wave you will encounter sections of the wave that are hollower and therefore quicker, and sections that are flat and full making them slower. If you are well ahead of the breaking wave you will

use a cutback. When you are in the critical section and you approach a slow section, stall the board to allow the wave to hollow out in front of you. Also, when a slow section is ahead the wave will flatten out or even start to break in a feeble fashion so you can use the speed being generated from your position in the hollow part of the wave to hit the flat spot and bounce off. This can be used in conjunction with a cutback.

RE-ENTRY

If a walling wave has a close-out section in the wall and you happen to be in a trim position, you are going to get knocked off your board by the lip or white-water as it breaks. In order to avoid this you can drop to the bottom of the wave. Picking an imaginary impact point, swing the board up into the lip or white-water and, as the wave breaks, make contact with the breaking wave. This enables you at the same time to use the wave's power to turn the board around and come back down the wave and out on to the next section. To perform a re-entry type of manoeuvre again requires practise and you will not be able at first to do much more than drop down the face into a bottom turn and bring the board around so the nose is pointing back up the wave. To start with you will not be able to get the board around in a much tighter turn than about 45°, though this is enough to pull off the manoeuvre.

Do not become despondent when your attempts to bring the board back over end up with you getting pitched off the board by the cascading lip of white-water because it is possible to analyse what is probably going wrong. Once your rear foot pressure is applied to the inside rail when coming off the bottom, there is a point of exit out of the turn and up onto the white-

Right: Driving the board hard up the wave, this surfer has a choice of either continuing the ride and performing an off-the-top move, or aborting the ride by kicking off.

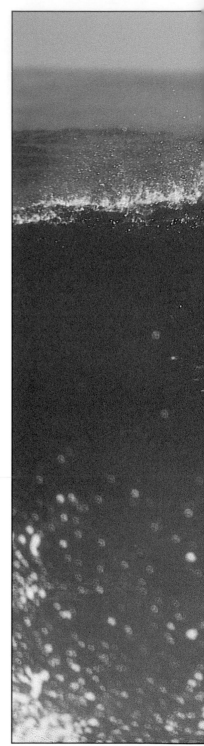

water. Once that point is passed and your foot pressure is applied to the outside rail, the board digs in down the entire length of the rail. This leaves the bottom of the board facing the collapsing white-water. Consequently, when the white-water hits your board (which by now is bogged down on the outside rail) it knocks you off. To start with, practise this manoeuvre at the end of a ride on the final section as the wave closes out. Once you can gauge the exit point from the bottom turn, and the weight transferrence from the inside to outside rails, and aim the board up on to the white-water to bring it back down again, you have the basics worked out. It is just what the name implies, a method of re-entering the wave via a breaking section.

ROLLERCOASTER

This is similar to and uses elements of the re-entry manoeuvre. It is commonly used to coast over sectionsof broken white-water that are not as steep and threatening as those requiring the use of a re-entry. Once you have mastered the technique of performing top-to-bottom man-oeuvres, combined with climbing and dropping, the board is worked in and out of various trim bands on a wave face and the roller coaster becomes a useful way of hopping over flat white-water sections. When you are riding a wave you have to anticipate whether or not to hop over the section or drop down around the sectioning wave. The advantage of going over the section is that you can get back into a good trim position far quicker utilising the section rather than skirting below it, because the route around it is far greater in distance. Once around the section, you still have to drive your board hard along the base of the wave and up on to the wall. This is a problem because the amount of forward driving speed lost covering

Right: Burleigh Heads, Australia. Although it looks safe it is hard to get out off the point and the surfer must ride down the point to the beach.

Above: A shore break or beach break at Hossegor, S.W. France; ideal for beginners breaking close to the shoreline.

Below: a point break that actually breaks on to a steep cliff face. It is extremely difficult to get out at this point.

the distance around the section will often not leave you with enough speed to get up into the trim position for the next manoeuvre.

The way to perform a rollercoaster is best described in stages. Once into a good speed trim position, look down the line of the breaking wave. You should be in the pocket of the wave in front of the breaking section of pitching white-water. As the wave starts to form and feather further down the line you may prematurely start to either pitch or roll down the face. The wave is not about to close out down its entire length but because the contour of the sea bed may be slightly higher at this point it causes the wave to think it is time to break. Once the wave has travelled over this high spot, the wave backs off, but the broken section still remains, which I have to deal with. Incidentally, I have only used the example of the sea bed contour changing but there are other reasons that make waves section,

such as backwash or waves hitting an irregular sea bed structure. As you approach the section you must anticipate how far down the wave the section will pitch or roll. If the section is going to back off then you can drive the board hard at the base of the section and punch through out on to the wall again. If the section is going to completely block your line down the wave then you must apply pressure to the outside rail, dropping your board out of trim towards the base of the wave. Whilst doing this you must pick the point you want to impact the bottom of your board off the section. Once this has been decided then you have to change the direction of the board to get it up on to the white-water. The pressure is released off the outside rail. Your body weight is now placed on the inside rail and you swing your board upwards on to the white-water. Once your board hits the point of impact, again transfer pressure to the outside rail to bring

Above: The classic set-up, an outside heavy breaking wave for the experts, and a mellow breaking wave for someone with less ability.

the board back down with the sectioning wave. From here your board can either be brought down parallel with the section or the nose can be swung around towards the beach on impact. (This I must hasten to add is far more difficult to do than coming back down square to the wave.)

Using the first method you will have to make a slight trim adjustment to get into a position for your next manoeuvre. Using the second and more difficult method, once you have successfully turned on top of the sectioning wave and are pointing towards the beach, you can drop with the section as you would when performing a bottom turn. Once you reach the bottom of the

SURFING AT YOUR ABILITY

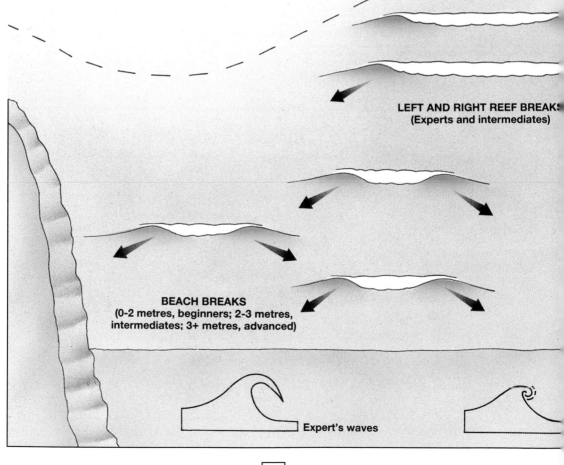

LEFT AND RIGHT REEF BREAKS
(Experts and intermediates)

BEACH BREAKS
(0-2 metres, beginners; 2-3 metres,
intermediates; 3+ metres, advanced)

Expert's waves

Left: The Northern tip of Lanzarote in the Canary Islands. Here you can see both reef and beach breaks 1,000 ft below, which are only accessible by boat.

Below: Here we have created the ideal surfing location: A point break peeling right, a rivermouth sand bank with left and rights, an outside reef left and rights, and a beach break with irregular sand banks peeling right and left.

OUTSIDE POINT BREAKS
(Experts only)

INSIDE POINT BREAKS
(Experts and intermediates)

LEFT AND RIGHT SAND BANKS
(Intermediates and beginners)
Beware of rip

eginner's waves

wave you can then place pressure on the inside rail to turn the board hard off the bottom and back into the surfing line of the wave. The great advantage here is the speed gained by dropping with the section when you turn off the bottom of the wave and it projects you further down the wave. The burst of speed allows you to thrust your board into the next manoeuvre rather than coax your board back into trim, as you would have to do if you used the first method.

Now that you know about the critical section to re-enter back into the wave, and premature breaking section to rollercoaster, I think it is time to discuss how to link these manoeuvres together. If you watch a surfing video of the top competition surfers you will see that the board is constantly being changed from one rail to the other. The waves have every last morsel of energy sapped out of them by the surfer "pumping" the board along the wave face. Some surfers such as Tom Curren seem to travel much quicker than others, finding speed all along the waves not just in critical power sections. This is accomplished by pumping the board from rail edge to rail edge. Air is flowing

Above: A lefthand point break. This wave is hard-breaking and very demanding, definitely not for the beginner.

Below: A gentle beach break, not so demanding and easy to catch, where a beginner can practise all the manoeuvres.

under the board and the board planes across the water much more quickly. When you learned the basic disciplines of surfing, a simplified form of rail-to-rail transition was useful when you wanted to keep the board moving between manoeuvres. The board, through a series of slight weight transferences from outside to inside rail is forced up the wave or down the wave in the trim band on the wave face. This manoeuvre can be instituted once

the angle take-off becomes second nature. As you drop at a comparative angle to the wave you can place pressure on the inside rail through your back foot to go up the wave, and through your heel on the outside rail to go down. At first you will only move a few degrees out of straight, but with practise as you try to perfect the other basic disciplines the inside-to-outside rail pressure, combined with upper body movements transferred down through the

legs, will swing your board up and down the waves between manoeuvres.

So let's recap these moves and look at what you are about to attempt. First, let me again remind you of safety, it still applies. Red Flag – no surfing, always surf in the designated surfing area. The drop in rule – remember to check before taking off that the wave is yours and there are no surfers on your inside against the peak. Then select the wave, angle your board in the direction the wave is breaking (left or right), catch the wave, stand up and get into the trim position on the wall. Adopt a proper surfing stance, knees slightly bent and keep your body loose. Do not adopt a fixed stance and tense your body up. The secret is to stay loose and feel the deck of the board through your feet. Move your back foot, put pressure on the tail, feel the direction your board wants to travel, and flow with it using your front foot to guide it. Try to swing the board up and down the wave in a climbing and dropping series of moves. Once you can angle take-off and ride along the wall, pull the angle you take off further around to the beach. Drop to the bottom of the wave to turn. Re-

Above: Sometimes a surfer has to paddle from rocks. This is dangerous because he or she may get caught by a set.

Below: A typical ding from a collision with rocks or another surfboard. The skin has been punctured, and needs drying.

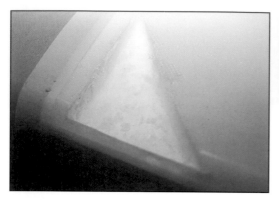

Above: With a sharp blade, cut out the damaged fibreglass and foam and make a neat hole for the new foam.

Above: Take a piece of foam, shape it to fit the hole you have cut, and make a tight fit to avoid air escaping when laminating.

Above: Cut a piece of glass fibre to the shape of the repair area allowing an overlap onto the surfboard.

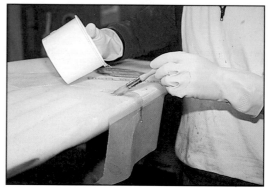

Above: The glass fibre should be held in place while you are applying the resin to the glass fibre with a brush.

lease the momentum you have gained by dropping down the wave when you turn, then project or drive your board hard out of the turn. This will thrust your board forward. The burst of speed can carry your board up into a fast trim position under the lip. If the lip is sectioning, try to use the power from the turn to hit the lip and swing the board around and down into another bottom turn. If the wave sections and starts to crumble over the face, try to keep the throttle open and drive the board up on to the foam or white-water and come back down with it. All the time between manoeuvres keep the board moving from one rail to the other. This level of competence will

take time to perfect and as time goes by you will learn to string together the moves both forehand and backhand. The ultimate aim is to use all the wave face and come hard off the bottom and smash the board off the lip. At first it will seem light years away but to coin a well-used and much-loathed phrase: Go for it!

DING REPAIR

When you can styllshly perform all the basic elements with a degree of confidence you will be trying to impress and to compete hard for waves. The surfboard you started out on has served its purpose but

now it is time for a change. However, before your trusty old tube shooter is traded in or passed down to your younger brother, it has one last useful part to play.

At the beginning of this chapter I mentioned that your board would be showing signs of wear and tear. If not just about utterly destroyed, this piece of equipment is a prime candidate for a refurbishment, so we are going to take a look at methods of repair. I know there will be those who cannot be bothered to fix up their board and prefer to let the experts handle the job. Surfboard factories will carry out repairs but it takes them time and after a few days of good waves they can be busy.

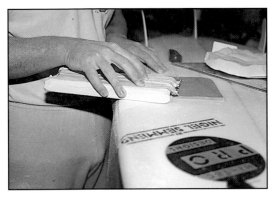

Above: Fix the foam into the hole and cut it off flush with the board and shape the dinged area into a slight depression.

Above: Having shaped a depression in the foam, rough up the surrounding area with sandpaper.

Above: With the brush work the resin into the glass fibre until it becomes transparent. This may take several minutes.

Above: When the glass fibre is sufficiently saturated with resin, level out the glass and resin in the depression.

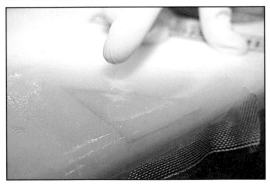

Above: Before the resin mixture starts to gel, level the repaired area with the board and check for air bubbles around the repair.

Above: Once the repair has set to a rubbery state, apply a sanding coat. Once this has set hard, sand and gloss.

CHAPTER 6

ADVANCED SURFING

The time has now come to buy a new surfboard. If you followed the advice in chapter 5 you will have fixed up the dings in your old board. Depending on your DIY skill, your board should be worth approximately half the amount you paid for it in the first place. There are various ways of disposing of your old surfboard: sell it privately, trade it in, or if another member of your family has been hit by the surfing bug you could if you are feeling generous hand it down to them. Unfortunately, the cost of new surfboards varies enormously around the world, depending on where you are surfing, so I am unable to advise on prices. Like learning to surf, there is a good deal of technique involved in buying a new surfboard.

get a better deal because it is good business to look after a valuable, regular customer. Do not be afraid to drive a hard bargain as half the fun of buying a new board is in the bartering over the trade-in price. Because the profit margins are not that great on a new surfboard it is highly unlikely that a good factory with a full order book will even discuss reducing the price of a new board, but on the other hand your old surfboard holds a higher profit margin so it is worth a little horse-trading.

If you do not have the facility to trade your board back to the factory you first got it from, and you have not built up a relationship with a retail outlet, it is always a good idea to look around the beach at what

other brands of board surfers ride. Now that you can surf and have been accepted by the regular surfers ask their advice, get a few suggestions, and shop around.

You may choose to ignore the following and go for the cheapest new board you can find. This is fine if you are satisfied with a mass-produced "Taiwanese junk stick" or a "backyard special", but both you and your surfing will suffer in the long run. It is an expensive mistake and eventually you will be hit hard in the pocket when you realise that your board is falling to bits and nobody wants to buy it or trade it in for better equipment. Unfortunately, there has been a flood of cheap surfboards on the market at a seemingly attractive price when in reality they are poorly

CHOOSING THE RIGHT BOARD

The problem that most surfers face when they go to the surf shop or factory to order their new surfboard is choice. In this situation you will be confronted with row-upon-row of gleaming, new custom surfboards. The choice is overwhelming. You may only be choosing a custom board, but the number of different designs is infinite, with a multitude of variations on each theme.

There are many good reasons why you should start your search for a new board at the factory or surf shop where you purchased your first board. During the period you have been learning to surf, the factory or surf shop will have supplied you with various pieces of equipment such as leashes, wax, and other accessories. By conversing with the staff you will have built up a friendly rapport and they will have kept track of your progress. If you are fortunate enough to live in an area close to the shop or factory the staff may well have seen you in the surf and may therefore be willing to offer you some constructive advice on your new board. Trading-in your board with the same company you bought it from means that you may

THE HIGH PERFORMANCE SURFBOARD

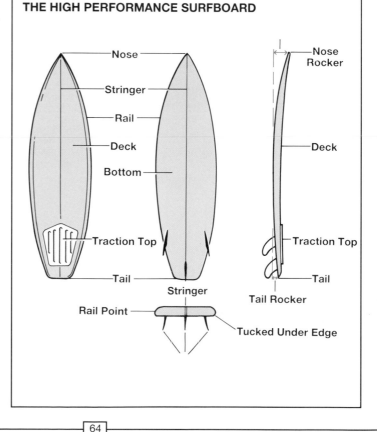

made imitations of real hand-crafted custom surfboards. Factories in the Far East mass produce look-alikes dressed in flashy decor that hides imperfections in the blank, and the board is buffed to a super-high gloss. In some cases these boards even carry reputable brand names when they are not even produced under franchise and are nothing more than fakes.

You should be spending your money on the expertise of a shaper who is capable of tailoring a surfboard to your height, weight and level of skill. the decor is of secondary importance.

Ordering your board
Once you appreciate the importance of using a reputable surf shop or factory the next step is ordering your board. First, it is very important to consult the shaper. He will have experience gained through shaping surfboards for hundreds of other surfers like you who are about to move up to their next board. He has to know how well you have progressed on your first board so take your board along with you. He will then advise you on the refinements necessary for you next surfboard. He knows the basic shapes that ride surf best in your local area. If you surf on one particular beach he can blend together a board with characteristics that will surf well on that beach. The board will also be ideally suited to your body dimensions and level of skill. This is the standard of service you expect for your money. In far-off Taiwan the shaper or shaping machine that churns out surfboards has obviously not got any idea about the conditions you will be surfing in so you will not receive the appropriate board.

The shaper will suggest an overall plan shape, length, width and thickness for any type of board. After discussing your needs with him you may decide that a **thruster** is the board best suited to your needs.

Below: A competition model surfboard that has stingers or wingers cut into the rails. These allow the board to have a combination of a wider plan shape being drawn in quickly with the cutout to a narrow tail.

This design was originally conceived by the Australian Simon Anderson and it has now become universally accepted as the shape of the 80s. Surfed by both recreational and contest surfers alike, the three-finned thruster design enables surfers to perform the top-to-bottom slashing manoeuvres that are popular in style today. This board allows you to positively direct it at points of impact and it is highly responsive to changes of direction, unlike other designs such as the twin-fin which is very loose, skating around in the tail and thus making directional surfing quite difficult.

Once you and the shaper decide on a final plan shape for your board you then have to take into consideration other factors. You must always remember that you are buying a high performance piece of equipment. It will take far less punishment than your first surfboard as the fibre-glass membrane that covers the board is much lighter. Your new board has to be light to perform well. If it had a heavy

glass finish it would not be as responsive.

Channels may be put in the bottom of the surfboard to aid the water flow to the final release or point of exit. You may also decide to have **wingers** or **stingers** in the rails. These cutouts are very vulnerable points so when placing your order go through the fine tuning items with the shaper and if you both agree to eliminate the ultra-high performance features go for a practical overall plan shape that can be easily maintained.

At this stage it is worthwhile talking to the laminator about the final weight of your finished surfboard. He can give you an ultra-light glass finish used by contest surfers, or a more pratical and conventional lamination with strengthening patches placed in key vulnerable areas. I would strongly advise that you opt for a slightly heavier glass finish with an extra tail patch, and if you have fin boxes then have an extra patch over them.

Even with extra glass the board is still very vulnerable to dings and stress fractures.

It is not unknown for modern, lightweight surfboards to snap in half while duck diving under waves, or in the event of a heavy wipe-out.

Below: A thruster tail set-up. Here you can see the use of stringers to reduce the width of the board in the tail section.

ACCESSORIES

Board bags

Because of the delicate nature of lightweight surfboards it is always a good policy to store and carry your board correctly. Board bags are available in various materials. For transporting your board to the beach on a bike or car a board sock is quite adequate for day-to-day protection. The sock has a reinforced nose and a draw string at the tail. It protects your board against knocks that cause fractures to the outer fibre glass covering the surfboard but is fairly useless against a major accident such as a board coming off the roof rack of a moving vehicle. The best protection against such damage is a ballistic nylon board cover that has a sandwich construction of ballistic nylon with heavyweight wrapping material

such as a bubble wrap in the centre. Covers such as these have to be able to withstand a fair amount of buffeting during travel, for instance during baggage handling at airports, to be of any use. Over the last few years manufacturers have perfected the technique of keeping surfboards safe from baggage handlers by building super-strong covers that will even survive the impact when a board comes off your car roof.

Nose guards

A relatively new accessory is the **nose guard.** During the last three years needle-nose surfboards have been developed with very sharp noses that are both dangerous to surfers and also susceptible to snapping.

Above: To perform radical manoeuvres like this you must use a light, highly responsive surfboard. Freedom of body movement is essential so your choice of wetsuit is just as critical as your choice of surfboard.

The nose guard is a bumper that fits around the nose protecting the board without hindering the board's hydrodynamic performance.

The tip of the nose is sheathed to protect the surfer from being impaled as happened once to a former World Champion!

Left: When it comes to difficult terrain a durable board bag is a must. This rap-pac will hold three surfboards, wetsuits and accessories.

Wetsuits

Now that you are moving into the high performance surfing division you need to study all aspects of pulling off radical surfing manoeuvres. This involves not only new surfboards, you will also need to study personal mobility and flexibility. Body movement restricted by tight and heavy wetsuits will cut down your ability to perform manoeuvres. Every ounce of energy has to be transferred through your body down into your board to project it into the critical areas of the wave. If your suit is constructed of thick neoprene you will be carrying heavy unwanted water trapped in the cells. A surfer has to strike a happy balance between keeping warm and having total freedom of movement. High performance wetsuits are available from all leading manufacturers around the world. These suits are constructed with total mobility in mind but not at the expense of thermal protection. Consequently, suits are constructed in different combinations: long legs with short arms, known as a short sleeve steamer; short legs with short arms, known as a spring suit; and for the surfer who requires to just keep the wind chill off his or her body, neoprene vests and Lycra rib skins are available. Wetsuits are made in different thickness combinations to achieve the maximum freedom of movement. Like surfboard makers some manufacturers offer a service where you can have your suit tailor-made to your requirements.

ADVANCED SURFING MANOEUVRES

Moving on from the intermediate surfing level to the performance of more radical manoeuvres requires the same amount of skill and dedication that learning the sport initially required. Indeed, some surfers never progress past the basic stages of the sport. Some people are very quick to learn to surf and continue to make rapid progress at all levels, while others only get there through sheer hard work and many hours dedication.

Unfortunately, local levels of surfing skill limits the amount of progress you can make. If you want to get any better then you need to travel to surf with the surfers who set the standard you wish to attain.

Let me explain this in another way: If we take a surfer who has learnt all the basics of catching and surfing waves and he is considered the best surfer on that beach, and he was to travel to California, Hawaii or Australia and spend one year surfing with the locals in any of those countries, then he would return home surfing to a much better standard than if he had surfed for the same amount of time on his own beach. The year spent in more skilled company would have pushed him to try harder than if he had surfed alongside his friends. This sometimes works in reverse. For instance in Britain in the early 80s local surfers saw for the first time world stars Shaun Tomson, Cheyne Horan, Wayne "Rabbit" Bartholomew and Derek Hynd. For years up until this time the standard of surfing had remained the same. Surfers watched these world class surfers performing monoeuvres that they had never before seen carried out in British waves.

With constant visits from top overseas surfers such as these the standard of surfing in Britain made a dramatic improvement.

The logical conclusion is that the more you come into contact with better surfers, the quicker you will learn, and the higher the standard of surfers you surf with, the higher your standard will become.

To start with you need to learn an efficient method of getting through waves without the hassle of bashing through white-water while getting a constant battering from breaking waves. The duck dive, once perfected, will in the majority of situations get you through the waves.

THE DUCKDIVE

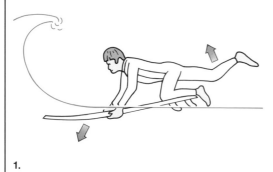

1.

2.

Surfers use this to avoid the full power of the breaking wave by tucking the board under the wave. When you have perfected this manoeuvre you will be able to paddle through the breaking waves with relative ease.
1. Anticipate the approaching wave and pick the point to submerge the nose. This has to be correctly judged. Too early or too late will result in a battering from the wave. Paddle towards the wave and pick a point at the bottom of the wave that is

The manoeuvres that we will be examining closely in this chapter are the **Bottom turn, Off-the-lip, Rebound cutback, Floaters** and **Tube riding.** These manoeuvres are in a logical order from take off, but you do not necessarily have to learn to perform them this way. Modern surfing consists of hard off-the-bottom turns, projecting the board up into the lip and then rebounding the board off the lip back down the face into the next manoeuvre. This lip attacking style is in complete contrast to the style of the 70s where flowing cutbacks and tube riding were considered "radical moves". The ultimate place on a wave is still deep in the tube; the styles of the 70s and 80s still have this in common and I would hazard a guess that even in the late 1990s, when

Above: Paddling out through waves when in close proximity to others. Hang on to your board in case you get caught inside by a sneaker set.

surfing will be filled with far more radical manoeuvres than now, the "green room" will still be the place to pull off manoeuvres.

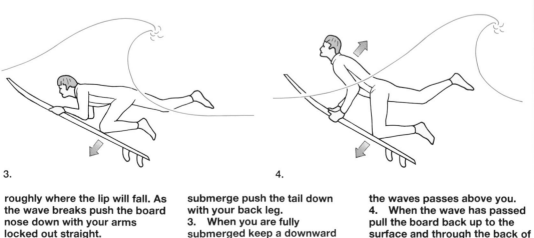

3.

4.

roughly where the lip will fall. As the wave breaks push the board nose down with your arms locked out straight.
2.   Once the nose starts to submerge push the tail down with your back leg.
3.   When you are fully submerged keep a downward pressure on the tail as the lip the waves passes above you.
4.   When the wave has passed pull the board back up to the surface and through the back of the wave.

Duck dive

In chapter 4 we looked at the different techniques for getting your surfboard from the beach to the line-up and concluded that for beginners it could very much be a matter of trial and error. Now that you have been surfing for a period of time and observed other surfers' techniques of pushing through waves, you will have tried to follow their example.

The duck dive is similar to the way certain sea birds handle the breaking surf. A lightweight bird will find it almost impossible to make its way through a mountain of churning white-water, but Cormorants and certain other sea birds have developed a technique of getting under the major force of the break-

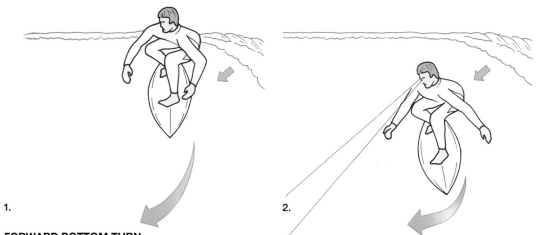

1.

2.

FORWARD BOTTOM TURN

1.   Dropping into the wave drive hard to the bottom to gain maximum speed.
2.   Enter into the critical area of the wave, pick the exact spot to perform the manoeuvre and at the same time drop your centre of gravity and push the board as far down the face as possible to extract the last bit of power.

3.   At the exact spot you have picked, exert pressure on the inside rail. The rail bites hard into the wave so transfer your upper bodyweight to pivot the

1.

2.

BACK BOTTOM TURN

1.   Dropping with the wave you have to pick your point to start. As with all backhand manoeuvres at some stage you are blind to what the wave is doing.

2.   Having assessed your speed and position on the wave start to place pressure on the inside rail, finely adjusting the board in relationship to the point where you will perform the turn.
3.   Where you have chosen to perform the bottom turn, exert pressure down onto the inside rail with your rear foot. The

ing waves. Surfers have since adopted this technique and modified it for their own use. Firstly, the nose of the board must be submerged. Then, push the nose down and further sink your board. As the wave rolls down to meet you, your board is tucked under the white-water and as the wave rolls over you, the nose is pulled up and you will pop through the back of the wave. The art to the duck dive is in the timing.

Getting your board totally submerged before the white-water strikes is essential. Just as you dive under a wave when surf swimming to avoid the mass of the waves, instinctively you surface once the wave has passed overhead. It is the same with duck diving and it

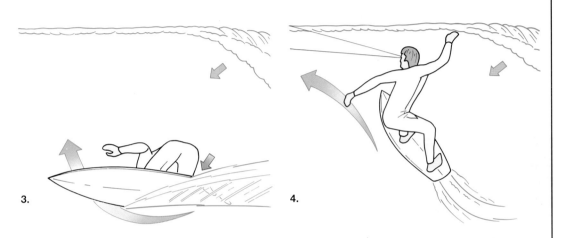

3.

4.

board around. The harder this is done the more power generated.
4.   The power from the hard-off-the-bottom turn is used to project the board back up into the lip. You then pick your point of impact with the lip. The whole idea is to drop down vertically, pivot the board off the bottom as tight as possible, and travel back up the wave face as vertical as the amount of speed generated with the turn will allow, and into the next series of top-to-bottom moves.

3.

4.

board cuts into the wave and the outside fins are released by using your upper bodyweight to pivot the board around on the tail. You can make contact with the wave with your hand to create another pivot point.
4.   When you release the board from the turn you then pick the point to drive the board vertically using the speed generated by the turn. The board must be driven hard vertically into the lip to deliver enough power for the next manoeuvre.

becomes second nature to paddle straight out through the surf using the duck dive. Of course there will be times when the waves are too intense or too big and you will get caught inside, but for general surf conditions, the duck dive is used by surfers to return out to the line-up through breaking waves.

Bottom turns

There are many alternative ways of turning your surfboard after take-off and usually you will need to make a split-second decision on the method of turning as you are paddling and catching the wave. As the wave forms you will assess whether you can drop and project hard off the bottom. If the wave becomes critical and the take-off is late you may decide to top turn then drop into a secondary bottom turn and project off the bottom. Alternatively, you may have to angle take-off, top turn and rebound off the lip, drop back down the face and then project off the bottom of the wave. There is a distinct advantage of dropping down the face of the wave and cranking your board around hard. Not only does it give a surfer a great feeling on big waves when you rocket off the bottom, it also allows the wave to wall up down the line, putting you in a position where you can use the face of the wave at its most critical point to pull off a series of top-to-bottom moves. If the wave starts to pitch out and tube, you can trim and stall and attempt to put yourself inside the wave. Simple on paper but hard in practise!

In very big waves you have to drop to the bottom and turn, because if you were to attempt to turn high in the wave, the fins of the board would spin out as the wave face hollowed. You would lose all forward momentum, side-slipping down the face. A classic example of this can be seen in videos and films of surfers riding big waves in Hawaii.

The purpose of the bottom turn is to gain as much momentum as possible. When dropping down the face your board is cranked around hard and you need to fix an imaginary point of impact in the most critical section of the lip. The speed that is generated whilst dropping down the

Top: Dropping to a point where the wave ahead has formed into a critical pocket, Tom Curren drives hard into the bottom turn with force.

Middle: Releasing the power out of the turn Tom is slightly stalling his board to choose the point to impact off the lip.

Above: Driving the board hard up the wave face Tom Curren will be in a position to rebound off the top, using all the wave face in front of him to gain maximum momentum for his next series of vertical manoeuvres. He will drop down into a bottom turn and then into another off-the-top move.

Right: Tom Curren has dropped in backhand. He is holding his board back, allowing the wave to develop in front of him before continuing the manouvre.

Centre: The wave has now walled up enough down the line for Tom to bring his board hard off the bottom and drive up at the lip.

Bottom right: Driving his board vertical up into the top to perform his move, Tom is already picking the point where he is going to perform his next moves.

face is unleashed in the turn and the board is then projected back up the face to collide with the lip. At the same time you use the power of the lip to bounce the board off and redirect your board down the wave.

Off-the-lip

Powering out of a bottom turn and bouncing your board off the lip is not the only time you will use the pitching part of the wave. You will set up the off-the-lip manoeuvre on a wave that offers no other riding possibilities other than one big manoeuvre. It is important to be aware always of what the wave will do. When you take off you will instinctively string together manoeuvres as the opportunities present themselves.

Most surfers have a favourite manoeuvre or set pattern of manoeuvres. They wind up the board gaining speed along the wave by utilising the optimum trim position on the wave. Their big manoeuvre is a vertical off-the-lip re-entry back into the wave. Surfers like Martin Potter have taken this move to even greater extremes by driving hard up the face of the wave, through the top of the wave until they become airborne. This manoeuvre is called an **aerial.** Some argue that the aerial is totally unfunctional, as was the **360°.** Unfunctional or not, it is highly spectacular and a real crowd pleaser. These top-to-bottom surfing manoeuvres can be punctuated with others such as cutbacks.

Off-the-lip Sonny Garcia. The wave is sectioning into a closeout. Sonny has driven the board hard vertical up into the lip to a perfect impact point where he can pivot the board around the drop back down the wave with the white-water.

FOREHAND OFF THE LIP

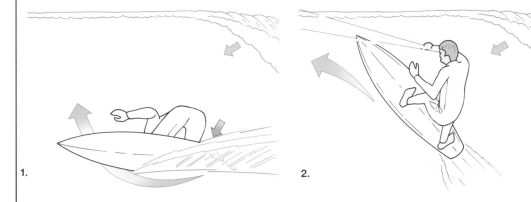

1.

2.

1.   In the tightest section drop to the bottom of the wave turning off the inside rail by placing pressure down on the inside back rail as in a bottom

turn. The board is put onto the inside rail, releasing the outside and rear fins.
2.   Bring the board hard out of the bottom turn vertially up the

wave face to the point where impact is to take place. Adjust the board with your rear foot to hit the exact impact point.
3.   The board is impacted with

BACKHAND OFF THE LIP

1.

2.

1.   Dropping in front of the section, turn hard off the bottom in the same way you would perform your backhand bottom turn. Place your board on the

inside rail by applying pressure on the tail. You can also make contact by placing your hand in the wave to act as an extra pivot point, but this is not always

absolutely necessary.
2.   When driving out of the bottom turn, release pressure on the inside rail and use your rear foot to finely adjust the track up

Advanced cutbacks

When the wave face is blocked by a section breaking or by broken white-water, this can be used to rebound off and change direction as with the off-the-lip manoeuvre. This is sometimes set up and you will

purposely take off and go the wrong way. By this I mean that the wave may be a perfect peeling right and you will go left, dropping in and surfing towards the oncoming breaking wave. You will rebound the board off the white-water, changing direc-

tion to go right. Once you have the board pointing back down the line you can then perform the next manoeuvre in the critical part of the wave. Other forms of cutback are used in an effort to milk the last drop of energy out of a wave. You are

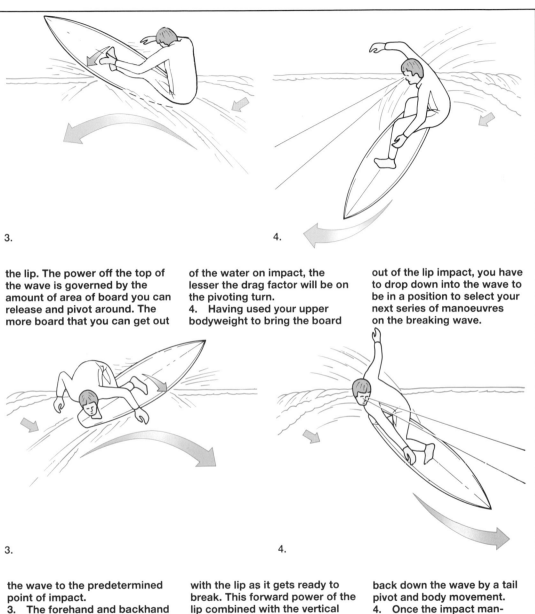

3.

4.

the lip. The power off the top of
the wave is governed by the
amount of area of board you can
release and pivot around. The
more board that you can get out

of the water on impact, the
lesser the drag factor will be on
the pivoting turn.
4.   Having used your upper
bodyweight to bring the board

out of the lip impact, you have
to drop down into the wave to
be in a position to select your
next series of manoeuvres
on the breaking wave.

3.

4.

the wave to the predetermined
point of impact.
3.   The forehand and backhand
off-the-lip is a glancing blow at
the lip. Your board has to collide

with the lip as it gets ready to
break. This forward power of the
lip combined with the vertical
trajectory of the board gives you
the power to redirect the board

back down the wave by a tail
pivot and body movement.
4.   Once the impact man-
oeuvre has been made push
the board down the face.

using the broken section as a bank
to bounce off. This allows you to
carve the board around changing
direction, so you can aim the board
back into the all-important critical
power pocket of the wave where
you will be ready to continue.

Floater

If a section of the wave is closing
out, but ahead of it there is a more
rideable face, you can bounce the
board off-the-lip coming back down
with it into the rideable part of the
face of the wave.

Tube rides

The tube of a wave is the ultimate
place to ride and requires a great
deal of skill. Certain surfers through-
out the history of the sport have had
what seems to amount to a second
sense and instinctively get tubed,

Right: Tom Curren has dropped in forehand. He is redirecting his board back off the lip down into his next set of manoeuvres.

while others are highly spectacular in their approach but rarely get deeply barrelled. For the average surfer getting tubed is a memorable and much talked-about moment, and so it should be. To set up a barrel and get in and out of the tube cleanly before it shuts down is what

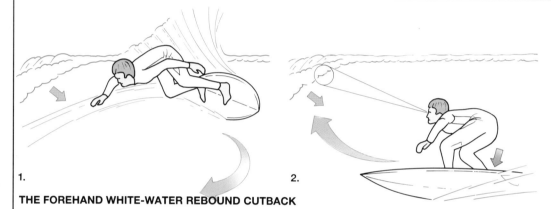

1.

2.

THE FOREHAND WHITE-WATER REBOUND CUTBACK

1.   Coming out of the critical section of the wave you may be faced with no other option than to cut back and allow the wave to develop in front of you. Place pressure down onto the rear inside rail. Your upper body and board are swung around so you and the board face the oncoming section.
2.   Select the point to hit the section while still pushing down

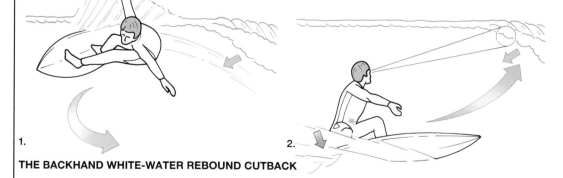

1.

2.

THE BACKHAND WHITE-WATER REBOUND CUTBACK

1.   The same applies as with forehand version of this manoeuvre. You are using the section around the critical pocket to allow the wave to form in front of you. Put the board into the first part of the S turn by foot pressure on the inside rail.

2.   Once you have secured the point of impact up on the white-water you have to control the board through your back foot,

surfing is all about.

Perfect surfing days are those when offshore winds gently hold up the waves as they tube over a shallow reef, compressing the air trapped inside and then blowing a fine water vapour out off the end of

3.

4.

on the inside rail. Then drive the board up the oncoming lip.
3.   Drive the board onto the white-water to a point where you

can pivot the board around on the tail through pressure on the outside rail.
4.   When you drop down with

the section you can assess how the wave has developed and started to section while you have performed your cutback.

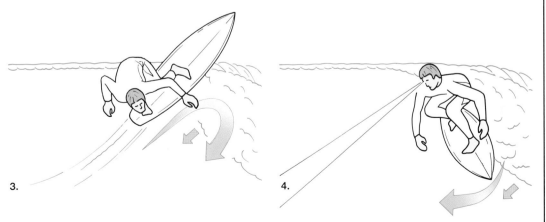

3.

4.

finely adjusting the board track up the wave face.
3.   On your backhand you have to pivot the board around on the

outside rail and guide the nose over and back into the downward descent with your front foot. This is the difficult

point of the manoeuvre.
4.   When you are in a descending track, pick a spot for the next manoeuvre.

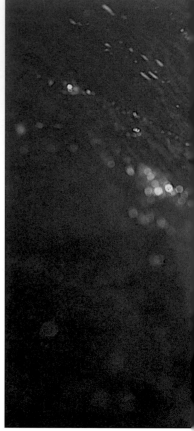

Above: The surfer here has to drop in, bottom turn, then pull up into the barrel. "Pipeline" in Hawaii is the perfect wave taking a special kind of surfer to ride it successfully.

Right: Barton Lynch in the ultimate position inside the tubing section of the wave. A good tube-riding technique is as important to learn as big off-the-lip manoeuvres.

1.

2.

TUBE RIDE

1.   Coming off the bottom you will need to assess the wave as it starts to develop. You can "set-up" a tube ride by bringing your board up off the bottom turn. Deliberately avoid the vertical track up the face. Hold back the turn by placing pressure on the inside rail with your back foot to let the wave start to form above you.

2.   Adjust your trim position by stalling with your back foot. From this point you can pull up into the tubing section to slow

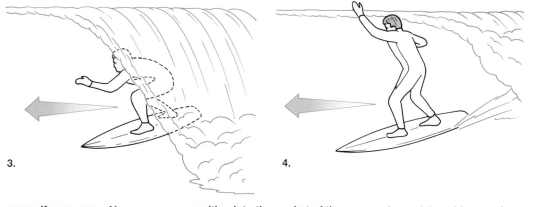

3.

4.

yourself even more. You can make contact with your hand in the wave face.

3. As the wave starts to pitch out over you, readjust your trim position into the pocket of the peeling wave and move your bodyweight forward to accelerate the surfboard.

4. Once you are clear of the lip and out of the tubing section, you can either set up your next section for vertical manoeuvres or, if the wave allows, repeat the tube-riding manoeuvre.

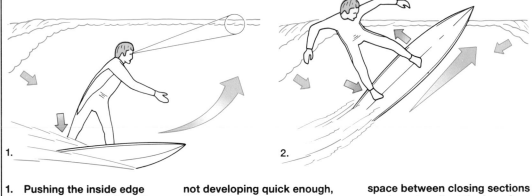

FOREHAND RE-ENTRY/FLOATER

1.

2.

1.   You have to decide when you are faced with a section whether or not it will be "makeable". Use it to rebound off and power through or drive your board over and back into the wave. This is where you will use the re-entry or a floater. Coming off the bottom in the same series of foot manoeuvres used in the off- the-lip move, you can watch the section developing in front of you. As the lip starts to crumble, push the tail down with your back foot.

BACKHAND RE-ENTRY/FLOATER

1.

2.

1.   Pushing the inside edge down with your back foot, the board is tracked up into the sectioning wave. If the section is not developing quick enough, then the board has stalled by downward tail pressure.
2.   Driving the board up into the space between closing sections you have to adjust the board through rear and front foot pressure to allow you to get up

the tube when the wave collapses. It is not only a reef that produces these conditions. Waves that tube can be total top-to-bottom-barrells such as the "Pipeline" in Hawaii, where you will drop deeply into the wave and try to pull up inside the tube. Some waves break for considerable distances with tubing sections along the entire ride, for instance, in Jeffries Bay in South Africa. Beach breaks are often quite cylindrical and demanding. Often while you are riding a wave the sections that collapse in front of you will jack up and pitch out. If you are in the right trim position, you can stall your board to let this section pitch then release your board from the stall to put yourself under the lip and inside the wave.

Advanced manoeuvres are an extension of the basic surfing manoeuvres. They are more exag- gerated and performed in an aggressive manner to gain the maxi- mum speed and performance out of the wave. There are more manoeuvres to be derived from mix- ing parts of each wave.

This is how you string together a ride. However, if a long section of wave is about to close out and no amount of off-the-lip projection would carry your board back into the wave, it can be floated across

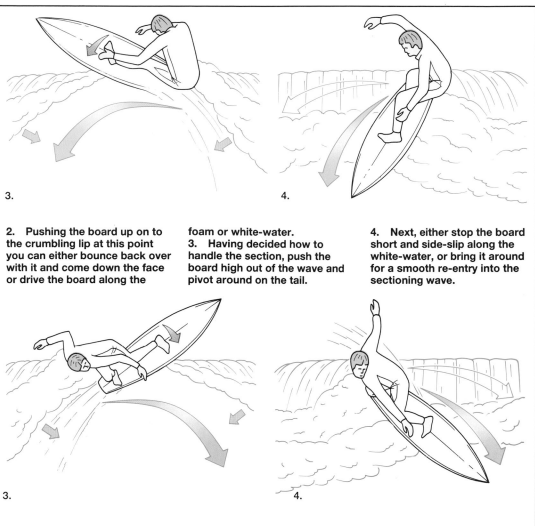

3.

4.

2. Pushing the board up on to the crumbling lip at this point you can either bounce back over with it and come down the face or drive the board along the

foam or white-water.
3. Having decided how to handle the section, push the board high out of the wave and pivot around on the tail.

4. Next, either stop the board short and side-slip along the white-water, or bring it around for a smooth re-entry into the sectioning wave.

3.

4.

on to the oncoming section.
3. The board is driven high up onto the oncoming section to either perform a floater across it,

or a re-entry descending with it.
4. You may choose to direct your board across the top of the white-water or foam and out to a

clear section in front. If the section is not "makeable" then you may choose to finish your ride with a re-entry.

the top of the breaking section if you wind it up to a maximum speed. Then you can float your board over the top of a long section of foam in a forward, side-slipping move, and then direct your board over the foam and back into the wave. Alternatively, the floater can be set up on a close-out wall and you can drive hard off the bottom into the closing lip and then float your board back down with the white-water.

RADICAL MANOEUVRES

To perform these you must learn to surf in the most critical section of the wave.

All the top professional surfers utilise this power pocket with vertical top-to-bottom high-speed manoeuvres. The idea is to stay either in this pocket or return to it to pull off manoeuvres. If you surf out

on the shoulder the power is minimal and vertical surfing is impossible. Your board will respond sluggishly and dig rails if the wave face is not steep. Do not be afraid to go for the big manoeuvres; try to surf deep with a commitment to making each manoeuvre work.

Top: When a surfer drops into a wave he or she instinctively assesses what the wave will do next before proceeding. In this instance Grishka Roberts has dropped backhand.

Middle: Having completed his turn Grishka stalls his board to allow the wave to develop into a hollow section.

Right: The wave is hollowing right down the line. Grishka pulls the board up under the lip while still slightly stalling his board, excessing total control.

The manoeuvres in this section, as in previous sections, will be practised and accomplished simultaneously as part of what goes to make up a complete ride. As you progress and learn manoeuvres, set patterns or formations will flow together. Always try to break the set routine; do not become predictable in your approach. When you can pull off radical, slashing manoeuvres – "surf to shock". Go for the big moves, set up a wave to pull off a series of top-to-bottom high-speed manoeuvres. Always be creative in your approach to each manoeuvre. While you are going through the more advanced stages of surfing you may start taking an interest in surfing competitions. There is no set level of skill required to enter a contest and if you are attracted to the contest scene, then the earlier you start entering the better. It seems that at the advanced level surfers choose one of two paths: contest, or travel and recreational surfing. Some are attracted to the lifestyle of one permanent summer travelling and competing around the world. This is only for the extremely talented. To achieve this lifestyle you require either extremely rich parents, or a sponsor, or a combination of both!

Above: Now the hollow section is starting to tube and the lip is pitching bodyweight has now got to be released from the tail to accelerate the board.

Below: Under the lip inside the tube, Grishka is still in control, making fine adjustments to his surfboard in order to maintain his position inside the wave.

CHAPTER 7

COMPETITION SURFING

How does a surfer begin a competition career? The usual way is through a local surf club affiliated to a national organization, which in turn belongs to the International Surfing Federation (ISF). In certain countries around the world, surfing associations co-exist alongside schools, colleges and universities and organise competitions.

AMATEUR SURFING

Local club events form the bottom rung of the ladder. From here a surfer will compete in regional or state contests for selection to the national teams. The ISF arranges world amateur contests that take place every two years with one of the member countries hosting the event.

Since 1980 it has been the practise for the winning World Champions to turn professional, which makes way for new amateur talent to emerge. Sponsors closely monitor the top amateurs and once the final world placings are decided the winner should be able to look forward to a lucrative sponsorship contract. The career of World Champion Tom Curren is a prime example of the way the system works: winning first the junior world title in 1980, the senior title in 1982, then turning professional and winning the world crown in both 1986 and 1987. Other world amateur champions however, like the 1980 World Champion Mark Scott, spent a year on the Pro World circuit and then retired.

PROFESSIONAL SURFING

The Association of Surfing Professionals (ASP) World Tour Events are the real prestige contests. These are staged around a world circuit that starts in Japan and finishes in Australia. The contests have major sponsors and the contestants are all compulsory members of the ASP. Winning prize money and gaining points in each event, most events are "A" rated, offering 1000 points to the winner. Some however are "AA" rated, offering 2000 points and increased prize money. The points awarded decrease by a percentage down through the placings. The Championship is decided on this basis, and at the end of the year the professional surfers have their best 75% of contest points totalled and the surfer with the most points on aggregate is the ASP World Champion.

The ASP World Tour is growing with more events and competitors participating each year. Currently the tour travels to such varied locations as Brazil, Japan, Hawaii, the East and West of Australia and America, Europe, and South Africa. As the popularity of the sport grows so has the ASP World Tour.

SURFING CONTESTS

There are two formats used during surfing contests. Firstly, the man-on-man format, with the winner progressing to the next round, and secondly the four-man heat format, with the first two progressing. The surfers wear coloured vests for identification and a judging panel, usually made up of five judges, scores their performances. A surfer is judged on how many successful manoeuvres he or she can perform in the critical part of the wave, losing points for deliberate interference with other competitors. Heats usually last for 20 minutes and the

Below: Jubilant Australian Gary Elkerton takes first place in the ASP Offshore Masters.

Right: Dave MacAuley from Australia is a stylish surfer.

surfers are allowed to catch ten waves in the allotted amount of time. From the ten waves, the best four are totalled together and the surfer with most first places on the judges' sheets is the winner.

There is no limit on the size or weight of surfboard used by the competitors. In most contests the surfers use super-light contest boards that have been finely tuned to suit local conditions. Most contest surfers will carry with them a number of surfboards for different sizes of surf and wave conditions.

Competition tactics

During a contest surfers select waves that will break for a long distance, allowing the rider to pack in a full repertoire of manoeuvres. They can only take off ten times in a heat, so once the rider's hands have left the rails on take-off it is considered a ride by the judges. The surfer may paddle for a wave and abort the attempt but his or her hands must not leave the surfboard. To decide who has the right of way on the first wave, a coin is tossed. The winner is awarded priority and can take off first on any wave he or she chooses. The other contestant is then allowed to catch a wave.

A priority buoy is used after this to decide who goest first on the next waves. Surfers must paddle around the buoy to gain the advantage of priority. Taking off first on the wave they choose, if a surfer takes off on the same wave as the surfer with priority then an interference or foul has been committed and the rider is penalised by either disqualification or by losing his or her highest-scoring ride. A surfer who catches a wave after the end of the heat is also punished in a similar manner. Contest surfers try to get four high-scoring waves that will allow them to surf all the way to the beach while performing as many manoeuvres as possible. Once they have managed to do this they start to build on their performance by pulling off high-scoring, radical manoeuvres.

All contest surfers wear waterproof watches and they are fully aware of the time they have left to catch waves. If they have priority they will play a cat and mouse game

with their opponent by letting the smaller waves go and choosing to wait for the bigger set waves. Because waves do not come in a regular sequence one surfer may have a distinct advantage at the start. If the second competitor does not get any good early waves, he or she is then under extreme pressure to pull back their opponent's advan-

tage. In this situation surfers abandon caution and go for radical manoeuvres to get back into the lead. In the finals of professional contests they use the best-of-three sets system. A surfer must win by two sets. This is very exciting for the crowd and on occasions when two evenly-matched surfers are fighting it out and one wins the first set, the

the period the surfing bodies were changing professional surfing policy. Mark Richards is credited with developing the radical twin-fin design that set the world of surfing alight in the late 70s and early 80s. Mark was often called "the wounded gull" because of his surfing style. He has now retired from professional surfing as a result of injury but still competes in Hawaii big wave events.

Tom Carroll

From Newport, Australia, Tom was a member of the extremely innovative "Newport plus" group of surfers in the early 80s. Tom is a tough little Aussie who surfs to the limit, and occasionally overstepping it, causing himself serious injury. His style of surfing is suited to both small and large waves, a fact borne out by his contest victories in many countries.

Tom Curren

Born in Santa Barbara, California, Tom continued his total dominance of world professional surfing by taking the title from Tom Carroll in 1986. Tom was destined to win the world professional title from the start. He won both World Amateur Junior and Senior titles in consecutive world contests. This quiet American rocketed through the established professional ranks with a display of aggressive surfing that has set standards for other surfers to follow.

There have been other notable contenders for the world championship crown. South African Shaun Tompson was one IPS champion who consistently reaches the final round of events. Shaun is probably most famous for his ability to be totally professional, an ambassador to the sport of modern professional surfing. Cheyne Horan of whom many said he could have been world champion if he had not experimented with changes in equipment. He was the surfer that most young surfers modelled themselves on in the early 80s. Wayne "Rabbit" Bartholomew, another IPS world champion has had a long and successful contest career. He was one of the first surfers to receive the total backing of the surfing industry.

Left: Tom Curren is the world's most successful surfer the sport has seen to date, winning Junior and Senior Amateur World Titles as well as the ASP World Crown two years running.

Above: The ASP have been quick to recognise the necessity to promote women's surfing. The world tour now runs a male and female division with both sexes competing for world titles.

crowd can get behind the other and lift his performance to bring it back to one set each. With everything depending on the last set the finalists pull out all the stops.

Because wave conditions vary around the world, the ASP use a minimum wave size. This is 0.5 metres (18 inches). Once the surf drops below this size the contest is adjourned until the surf size picks up again. What makes the world tour so interesting is the different venues for events. Some surfers are, for want of a better category, small wave specialists, while others perform better in big waves. Unfortunately for the big wave riders, most contests are held in small-to-medium size surf, 1 to 3 metres (3 to 10 feet). The premier events are those held in Hawaii; not because they award more points and prize money, but because they are usually held in big waves which are more demanding.

If a surfer gets an early lead on the world tour he can afford to choose his events because a quarter of his worst results are discarded. It is not unknown for certain top profession-

als to miss events, knowing that they can make up points with AA-rated contests that carry double points. The top 32 surfers in the world are seeded into the last rounds of a contest as happens in tennis tournaments. Up-and-coming surfers have to go through a series of trials or elimination rounds before the main event starts. As recently as only a few years ago trialists, with a few exceptions, rarely ever made it to the main event. Today, with surfers becoming world class at a much younger age, trialists quite often make it through into the main event and cause all kinds of upsets.

WORLD CHAMPIONS

Since the ASP took over from the IPS there have been three World Champions: Mark Richards, Tom Carroll, and Tom Curren.

Mark Richards

Born in Newcastle, Australia, Mark won the World Championship an unprecedented four times during

South African pro surfer Mike Burness surfing in the Lacanau Pro, France.

COMPETITION RIDING

We have created a contest ride to demonstrate the type of manoeuvres a competition surfer has to execute in the most critical section of the wave, for the longest distance, to score the maximum amount of points. Read from left to right . . .

Bottom turn . . .

Off the lip . . .

Pick the impact point . . .

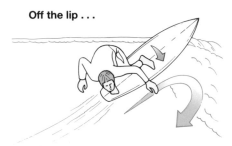

White-water rebound . . .

Floater/re-entry . . .

Picking point of impact . . .

Backhand white-water rebound . . .

The next manoeuvre off the top or cover up . . .

Bottom turn . . .

Cutting back . . .

Bottom turn under a section . . .

Impact point for floater/re-entry . . .

On the top into . . .

Slash back . . .

Cover up or tube ride . . .

Into the next set of manoeuvres . . .

CHAPTER 8

MALIBU SURFING

Surfboard lengths fall into different categories: Shortboards are between 170 to 200cm (5ft 8in to 6ft 8in); beginners' boards 200 to 225cm (6ft 8in to 7ft 6in); mini-Malibu 210 to 240cm (7ft to 8ft); modern Malibu 240 to 270cm (8ft to 9ft); and traditional Malibu 270 to 290cm (9ft to 9ft 8in). These lengths are a rough guide, though accurate enough for the purpose of reintroducing the Malibu back into the sport of surfing.

THE HISTORY OF MALIBU

The first surfboards constructed of foam and fibreglass were built in California in the late 50s. They were ridden at places like Rincon-Delmar, Redondo, Windansea, Tretles, and Malibu. For some reason the point break at Malibu lent its name to the surfboard and the name stuck. During the 60s the Califor-

nians were masters of Malibu riding. Names such as "Da-Cat," alias Mickey "Mr Malibu" Dora, the all-time anti-hero of surfing ruled Malibu with an iron fist. His battles with arch rival Johnny Fain for the "Mr Malibu" title were legendary, if not blown out of proportion. The Malibu era was a time in surf history when all the famous names were real characters who paddled out without leashes, on boards that weighed between 15 to 20 kilos (30-40lbs). This was a time when surfing was the graceful art of walking the board, hanging five and ten, with the drop-knee cutback being "the big manoeuvre."

As surfing evolved and boards got shorter the Malibu style of surfing gradually faded with the advent of the "rip and slash" era. For almost twenty years the art was only seen in California where surfers of the original era still rode Malibus.

Sometime in the early 80s at Bryon Bay, Queensland, Australia, there was a minor revival of Malibu-style surfing with super-light 285cm (9ft 6in) traditional Malibu surfboards. A new era was about to stårt. During the same period in California surfers were also turning their attention towards these traditional surfboards and it was not long before boardmakers started pulling out old templates and dusting down

Right: Peter Lascelles not only shapes modern Malibus in Europe, he also test rides them in perfect trim at Jamco del Agua, Lanzarote.

Below: Modern Malibus are both light and extremely more manoeuverable than those of twenty years ago. This is an epoxy and polystyrene model.

old surfing heroes to put them back in the limelight after 20 years in the wilderness – names like Rusty Miller, now in his mid-forties, has become a star on the new Australian Malibu contest circuit.

Of course, there is a big financial incentive for the surfing industry. Two generations of surfers have grown too old to ride short lightweight surfboards but with the introduction of mini-Malibus and traditional Malibus, older surfers have become re-enthused at an increasing rate each year. In fact the biggest growth rate in Australia in surfing products in 1987 was in the production of custom Malibu surfboards. These longer, wider surfboards are ideal for the surfer who has had a long lay-off; within a few days anybody who has surfed can jump on a Malibu and, providing they are in reasonable physical shape, can get back into surfing.

So apart from allowing old surfers to go on surfing longer who else rides Malibu boards? In certain coastal areas in California and Australia young surfers are becoming colt riders of modern Malibu surfboards. They are not only reliving the era by their choice of surfboard, they are taking the era into their lifestyle, dressing in 60s-style clothing and driving renovated cars of the period.

Malibu development
Since the reintroduction of these boards shapers have been able to utilise knowledge they gained from developing shortboards. Many refinements have been tried with some working well when incorporated into a Malibu. The three-fin thruster system allowed a longboard rider to tune his board to suit different wave conditions. The Malibu rider who has three fin boxes fitted can now enjoy the riding characteristics of a single fin, twin fin and thruster all in one surfboard.

The development of Malibus has split into three groups: the 210 to 240cm (7ft to 8ft) mini-Malibu; the 240 to 270cm (8ft to 9ft) modern Malibu; and the traditional 270cm (9ft) and longer Malibu. These boards have differed little in 20 years.

Mini-Malibu
These boards were to fill the missing link in the chain. The mini-Malibu allows a short board surfer to change from an ultra-radical style of surfing to the mellow flowing style of the 70s while retaining certain qualities they would use when riding a short board. There are those who think that riding a mini-Malibu adversely affects shortboard style, while other surfers, like Australian Derek Hynde who used a longer board to get back into surfing after a serious eye injury back in the early 80s, thinks differently. Derek was one of the most creative surfers of that period and people say that he was doing the same radical manoeuvres on a longboard as on his shortboard.

The mini-Malibu has extended a surfer's enjoyment of the sport. Before its invention surfers who were coming to the end of their surfing careers and not getting in the water on a regular basis due to business or family commitments found it hard to paddle and catch waves on a shortboard. Boards between 210 to

Above: The technique of paddling and catching waves is easier than on a short board. The extra area of foam makes the Malibu extremely floatable.

Above: Once the wave is caught in a late take-off the extra length can be a problem. To avoid this, take-off is more effective when slightly angled.

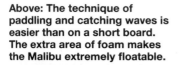

240cm (7ft and 8ft) with extra flotation helps the surfer get into the waves more easily. Because the Malibu boards have more physical area they are not thrown about quite as drastically as shortboards. With the new development in materials, for instance epoxy resin and polystyrene, foam board weights have now been drastically reduced. These super-lightweight boards are extremely responsive and over the next few years as good shortboard surfers start moving over to these new super-light boards we will see if they can push these boards to the limit. If development goes the same way as shortboards then the hydrodynamics will be finely tuned and the radical manoeuvres commonplace now on a 178cm (5ft 8in) thruster may, by the 1990s, be the norm on a mini-Malibu.

Above: The front half of the board is used for nose riding and trimming. Here Peter Lascelles is tucked under the lip in perfect trim position.

Modern Malibu

These are the next step up from the mini-Malibu boards. Probably the most popular of the new generation of long boards, they have to be ridden in the traditional style and once a surfer becomes used to riding, turning and cutting back, he can then start to introduce whatever element of shortboard riding he thinks will blend with the traditional style. Boards around 240cm (8ft) are ideal for fine-fin tuning. They respond extremely well when used as a single fin, multi-fin, strata-fin, and as a thruster when fitted with a wing fin.

Above right: The lightweight board makes it easy to adapt certain short-board skills. The board can be ridden tight to the critical section of the wave.

There are numerous fin designs for windsurf boards that work extremely well in Malibu boards. This is one area at least that surfing and windsurfing have common performance factors.

Traditional Malibus

These are the same length and width as the boards of the 60s, the only improvement being the weight factor. The board is constructed of lightweight foam with a balsa central stringer and laminated with varying weights of fibre glass depending on the final weight of the

board required. The 60s boards were decorated with mahoganay stringers, a laminated wood nose, tail blocks and wooden fins. All this woodwork looked great but it put the weight of the boards up to around the 20 kilos (40lb) mark. Today's traditional Malibu builders have so far stayed away from these wood decorations but it is only a matter of time before the recreators of the era start inlaying thin strips of timber into the foam and laminating mahoganay and balsa wood nose and tailblock. Incidentally the block of wood at the nose and tail were not just for decoration. The surfers of the 60s did not have leashes so when they lost their boards they had to swim back to the beach to retrieve them. The board would be washed over the rocks onto the beach. The nose and tail block

stopped the board from being seriously damaged. The emphasis today is on lightweight surfboards with hi-tech fin systems. Rumour has it that the Malibu fine tuners are planning to produce authentic super-light traditional Malibus with polycarbonate stringers and a kevlar coating weighing around 4 kilos (8lbs) – mind blowing!

THE TECHNIQUES OF SURFING A MALIBU

The same basic manoeuvres apply to Malibu surfing as they do to shortboard riding. After all they were all originally derived from longboard style. The bottom turn, trim, cutback and tube ride are all common to both types of surfing. Malibu riders have to walk around the board to achieve turns and accelerating,

whereas the shortboard rider does this with weight transference and body movement. Malibu surfing is defined on style and smooth flowing body actions rather than the top-to-bottom attack of shortboard riding. The one thing a Malibu rider cannot do is duck dive, unless of course he or she weighs over 110 kilos (18 stone)! The extra area of the board makes it impossible to sink. If the nose is sunk leaving the tail sticking out of the water the weight of the collapsing white-water of pitching lip can snap the board in half. Most Malibu riders use the eskimo roll to get through waves.

When a Malibu rider gets caught inside the breaking surf he or she will get washed a long way backwards, a distinct disadvantage of a long, highly floatable surfboard.

Bottom turn

The Malibu surfboard has a lot more area with greater flotation. Therefore to cut down the 'corky' flotation effect modern Malibus are made thinner than the traditional Malibus, which allows them to be dug into the turn to avoid drifting around. The board is turned from the tail so the further back the rider stands the harder the board can be turned, unlike the weight transference from rail to rail necessary on the shortboard. The bottom turn is long and drawn out. The board is not being projected back up into the lip, it has to be brought off the bottom into a good trim position. The rider, once in the trim band of the wave, can then walk forward to accelerate.

Now, this is where style comes into it. A longboard rider walks foot-over-foot, to shuffle up a surfboard is not on, just as much today as it was back in the 60s. When the board is trimmed high in the curl of the breaking wave and the tail of the board is covered by the breaking wave a surfer can stand on the nose and **hang ten** or **five** (a term that refers to the number of toes hanging over the nose). Because surfing today is a much more serious affair, manoeuvres such as **hanging one** and **brown eyes** are considered unfunctional and definitely uncool.

Nose riding and walking the board

The first three feet of the surfboard are used for nose riding; the middle part for trimming and setting up manoeuvres; and the back third is for turning and cutbacks. The ultimate aim of a Malibu rider is to turn hard off the bottom, walk foot-over-foot to the nose and hang ten screaming along the wave for 100 metres (100 yards) or so in this position. Just like shortboard riders Malibu riders have to get around sections of white-water that block the wave face. The Malibu cannot be turned from the nose while hanging ten so the rider, if he adopts the traditional style, must walk back to the tail to perform a cutback.

Alternatively, if the surfer has ridden a shortboard he or she can use a modified off-the-lip manoeuvre or a floater-type manoeuvre. Of course these are not nearly as radical as they are when performed on a shortboard, but authentic Malibu riders would shun the use of these "tooth-

Right: Setting up the manoeuvre – the board is put into a heavy tail stall giving the surfer time to carefully choose his position to attack the lip.

Below: The ultimate position for any surfer, short or longboard. Just inside the "curtain" in perfect trim under the lip and driving hard for the shoulder.

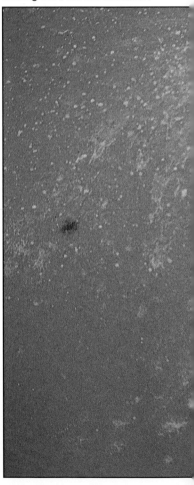

Below: Unorthodox maybe, but quite radical for a Malibu surfboard. This is a perfect example of a short board cross-over technique.

pick" manoeuvres. Once the surfer has dealt with the section he or she then re-trims the board and sets up the next nose ride.

In California in the 60s the surfers of the day would enter nose-riding contests. The surfer who could stay on the nose hanging five or ten the longest won not only the respect of everyone on the beach but would also take home a few hundred dollars and a trophy. These contests became very serious and fine tuning of boards became common.

Some surfers had concave noses on their boards, with the front 75cm (30 inches) of the board's bottom scooped out to a depth of about one inch rather like the inside of a spoon. The principal idea being that as the

Below: A good example of a traditional bottom where the surfer has taken the drop. He is sighting down the line of the wave before completing the turn.

board travelled down the wave with the surfer on the nose it was given more lift. Cunning surfers bolted wings to the fin of their board to stop the tail coming up out of the water. One surfer even went as far as laminating two house bricks to the tail in an attempt to counterbalance his weight on the nose! Still, the undisputed king of board nose-riding, David Nuuhiwa, rode a standard 300cm×50cm (9ft 6in x 22in) surfboard without modification. That was until surfboard manufacturers realised that if they put David on a modified model advertised in the magazine *Surfer* the whole of California would demand that model and that is how surfer sponsorship began. The nose-riding contest got so big that prize money increased to thousands of dollars and many of the competing surfers won cars, motorbikes and televisions.

Today the contests scene in both Australia and America is growing quickly to the disgust of many kneeboarders. A Malibu surfboard division was added to the 1988 Amateur World Contest as a permanent division at the expense of the kneeboarders. Each country entering the world contest was only allowed one kneeboard representative and a Malibu rider instead of two kneeboarders. The professional Malibu contest now attracts all the old stars: David Nuuhiwa, Corky Carroll, Rusty Miller, Nat Young, Flea Shaw and Herbie Fletcher, but the final seal of approval to the Malibu renaissance will only come when Mickey Dora once again challenges Johnny Fain to the "Mr Malibu" title. It would be interesting to see history repeating itself before the stars of the 60s finally fade into obscurity. In the near future Malibu surfing may reach unexpected heights of performance. The surfboard manufacturing industry has created a vacuum to aid sales of the high-tech longboard, they have had to indulge in a spot of reincarnation with the some of the old stars.

BUYING A MALIBU

Having talked about the history and variety of Malibu surfboards as they exist today, how do you go about buying one? At the moment unless you live in a major surfing country they are a rare commodity indeed. My advice is to write to your local Amateur Surfing Association (ASA) who will be able to put you in touch with either a manufacturer or importer. As with my advice on the technique of purchasing a shortboard the same applies to Malibus. The art of shaping a modern Malibu is far different from that of shaping, say, a 2 metre (6ft) thruster. Some shortboard shapers try to scale up a shortboard template to longboard

Below: Test them till they break. Before a company can commercially produce superlight Malibus, a vast amount of research and development has to take place.

Above: This super-lightweight board has been put back together for more trials to determine how to best strengthen production models in the future.

proportions. This is dangerous. A The Malibu is a board concept all of its own. It is like comparing wave-riding sailboards to surfboards. Although they are used for the same basic thing — riding waves — the technique of riding them is entirely different. The same thing applies to modern and traditional Malibus. So if you want to buy a longboard go to a longboard specialist who is experienced in constructing boards over 240cm (8ft) long.

The mini-Malibu as I said earlier is the link that connects shortboard riding to longboard riding and to some degree shapers can and will introduce shortboard features such as channels and wings to a Malibu. Be careful because the area is so new that few people really know what does and does not work. I can give you an example. I have been riding longboards for the last ten years. To start with I used an Australian 240cm (8ft) surfboard made by a longboard specialist in Queensland. Unfortunately I broke the board in half and when I went to my local surfboard factory to get a new one nobody knew how to shape one so consequently I had a series of scaled-up shortboards that were completely useless. Not until Australian Pete Lascelles, who incidentally, was a Queensland Junior Champion during the longboard era, started shaping authentic longboards did I get a decent board.

CHAPTER 9

TRAVEL

Surfers are great travellers. Once you have been bitten by the surfing bug you will want to ride as many waves as possible. If you live in a country with a severe winter then travelling abroad will form a major part of your surfing year. Of course not everybody can take off for the whole winter (although some surfers manage to do so, moving from the northern to the southern hemisphere to avoid cold winter waves). Most of us have to be content with a vacation, usually best taken to coincide with favourable conditions in other countries.

If you are planning a trip equipment is an important factor, especially taking the right board for the waves you will be riding. If you choose to go to a major surfing country such as America or Australia you could buy equipment there.

The ultimate surf trip is the "surf safari" which involves looking for unridden waves in remote regions of the world miles away from civilisation; camping under the stars on some remote beach or headland. This sort of trip takes careful planning and many things you take for granted at home have to be taken into consideration: medical supplies, ding repair kits, and spare equipment, for instance.

The world has many surfing countries with some being much friendlier than others. Local surfers are not pleased to see overcrowding caused by outsiders which is becoming a worldwide problem. This causes heavy localism, so you should consider this before planning a surf trip. In this chapter we are going to look at countries worldwide and take you on a surf safari to Lanzarote, but first we need to consider the essential equipment for the travelling surfer.

EQUIPMENT

If you are going to Australia, America, Hawaii or South Africa you will be able to purchase a board suitable for the waves in those countries once you get there.

Above: Paddling out, a surfer's eye view. Surfers travel to escape overcrowded beaches. These are ideal conditions, 3ft (1 metre) surf with only two out!

Taking a board with you can be a disadvantage, because the airlines do not like carrying them because of their bulkiness and they may be damaged badly. Also if your current board is not suited for the local conditions and you want to exchange it for a new one you will find the trade-in value very low.

So, if you are considering having a new board made to take on your trip then give it some serious consideration. It can work out much cheaper to buy a good secondhand board in your country of destination. If you are forced to take your board then a board bag is essential. Always wrap you board first in bubble wrap. Make extra sure the fins are protected. If you go to your local board factory they will supply you with some foam off-cuts that can be easily shaped into fin covers and

taped into position with masking tape. Once your board is wrapped in bubble wrap put it into your board bag and mark on the outside of the bag GLASS – TOP LOAD ONLY. This should stop your surfboard from being thrown around.

Wetsuits

These are another consideration. obviously in some countries you will not need a wetsuit because the climate is hot all the year round. Other countries may be cooler at the time of year you plan to surf so a lighter wetsuit may come in useful.

Ding repair kits

Always essential on a surf trip and because the kit contains inflammable resin and acetone it must be packed extremely well.

The kit should consist of fibreglass, foam off-cuts, pre-accelerated resin, catalyst, a paint brush, acetone, a spare fin if your board has fixed fins or if it has boxes, a spare fin and plate and screw. In addition, it is worth including a selection of various grades of

Above: Whether it's a rusty pre-1970 model or a ritzy model like the one above, a surfmobile has helped to get surfers to inaccessible parts of the world for the past 25 years.

wet and dry, sandpaper, a surform blade, stanley knife blade, hacksaw blade and stirring sticks. With these items you should be able to patch up your surfboard. A short-term remedy to minor dings is duct tape, which is strong and water-proof (this tough aluminium tape is used to tape over the joints in ventilation ducts so it is very reliable).

The repair kit can be packed with the surfboard between the fins and secured to your board with tape to stop it sliding about in the board bag when you travel.

Other essential equipment
Spare leashes, rail savers and wax. The grade of wax is important – if you are going to the tropics get the tropical grade. Winter wax is softer in cold climates and melts on the board in warm countries.

If you choose a tropical climate then you will need a sun block to stop your face and body getting scorched. Take a Lycra rib skin to keep the sun off your upper body until you get acclimatized. If you stay in the water too long in the tropics then you will suffer from sunburn. This is extremely painful and if your skin blisters the wound will take time to heal. Constant contact with salt water and more burning cause severe scarring and possible skin cancer. Always cover up until you get acclimatized to the intensity of the sun. Use zinc cream to protect your face and nose and do not forget to take a pair of good-quality sunglasses to block out harmful infra-red and ultra-violet rays.

Most surfers prefer to travel light, as a surfboard and ding repair kit well packed will take up about half the weight airlines allow you to carry as normal baggage. Any other equipment can be packed in a back-pack with your clothing. Do not take much with you; weigh it first to make sure that it is not overweight. Excess baggage is expensive.

TRAVEL ARRANGEMENTS

Visas
Contact the embassy representing the country you intend visiting. Find out from them whether or not you need a visa and if so how long it takes to get. If you are planning a long stay it may need renewing while you are away, so check how quickly this can be done. Also, find out how much money you need to gain entry to the country. Make sure your passport is current and will not run out while you are away. If you live in a country where you are not a nationalized citizen and you are there under the conditions of an entry visa make sure you will be allowed back into the country before you leave.

Insurance
Always take out medical and travel insurance. Make sure that your medical bill will be paid and you have the policy with you on your trip. The travel section of the policy may not cover your surfboard. If this is the case get a worldwide extension

to your household policy for the duration of your trip, making sure that your policy covers you for the replacement value of your surfboard. This is best done through an insurance broker who can advise you on what cover you can get.

Tickets
When you purchase your ticket make sure that the status of your ticket is marked "OK" in the appropriate box. A word of warning, if you have purchased a cheap ticket with stopovers find out the waiting time between planes as ticket agents will schedule your journey with two or more charters. Check the timing between flights, make sure you have enough time to transfer and the ticket status is marked OK. If it is not you could find that you sit around the airport as a stand-by passenger waiting for a spare seat. Allow plenty of time to check in before flights and inform the check-in desk that you want your surfboard TOP loading and that they tag it with FRAGILE GLASS tickets.

If you are travelling by boat or ferry the same basic rules apply. Allow enough time to check in: purchase your ticket well before your journey; and do not leave your surfboard on the roof rack – always put them inside your car or van. Some countries will only allow one surfboard per person on entry and may ask for a deposit that is returned on departure. Airport security in some countries is very tight and surfboards have been used in the past for smuggling drugs in specially hollowed-out chambers. I have heard of some suspect surfboards being sawn in half by over-enthusiastic custom officers. If you are subjected to heavy scrutiny point out to the custom officers that if a surfboard is placed in front of a strong light source they can see through it.

SPAIN AND PORTUGAL

If you travel on a European tour taking in France, Spain and Portugal, you will notice an immediate change in culture and language when crossing borders. Nowhere is this more evident than when you cross from France into Spain. The

Above: Matt Archbold, Grand Plage, Biarritz. The area around this French town is now generally considered to be the surfing capital of Europe.

Basque region has some of the most spectacular scenery in Europe, with the Pyrenees stretching from the Mediterranean to the Atlantic. The coastline of northern Spain has one outstanding wave, the river mouth at Mundacca. This lefthand breaking wave is a beach break that is constantly changing. After heavy rain the flood water from high in the Pyrenees runs out into the sea destroying the sand banks. Spain's other surfing areas are in the Canary Islands. The holiday islands of Gran Canary, Tenerife, Fuerteventura, and Lanzarote all have good, consistent winter waves. Lanzarote has reefs and points capable of holding very big swells.

The coastline from Oporto to Lisbon in Portugal is alive with small fishing villages. The cobbled coastal highways give way to the smooth tarmac road to Figuera Da Foz. This holiday town has excellent point and beach breaks. Further down the coast the port of Peniche has probably the best waves in Portugal, while Ericeria, north of Lisbon, is an accessible right-hand point break. Lisbon itself has several good beach breaks.

FRANCE

The Atlantic coastline of France has waves from La Torche down to Biarritz consisting of a variety of reef, point and beach breaks. The Continental shelf is shorter than around the British Isles and the waves tend to be slightly more powerful. The premiere areas stretch along the coast west of Bordeaux down to the Spanish border. In fact, the beach breaks of Lacanou and Hossegor are contest venues on the ASP World Tour.

Going south into the Biarritz area the coastline changes from long, flat beaches to coves and headlands. Biarritz has several excellent beach breaks such as Anglet, Grand Plage and Côte de Basque. Out of Biarritz the coastline winds in a series of points and coves that break on big Atlantic swells. For instance, Guethery, a right-hand peak in the middle of a bay, and Laffantania, a right-hand point break that is only a few kilometres from the Spanish border. The best months to visit France are April, May, September, October and November. June, July and August are usually fairly calm months. Most surfers doing the European tour follow the sun south from France into Spain, on to Portugal, and then either down to Morocco or across to the Canary islands in pursuit of excellent surfing conditions.

Above: Early October. This is typical of the waves that break in autumn along the French and Spanish coast between Biarritz and Mundacca.

BRITISH ISLES

Until the start of the 80s England was not even considered a surfing nation. However, with the new interest focused on professional surfing England has come to the attention of the surfing world by hosting the Surfmasters contest in Newquay, Cornwall. Because the southwest counties of Devon and Cornwall take the full force of the Atlantic swell Newquay is now considered the centre of the sport in the British Isles. Nevertheless there are many other areas where surfing is establishing a foothold. South Wales, Porthcawl, the Gower Penninsula, and Freshwater have some great beach and reef breaks. Eire and Northern Ireland also have unsurfed beaches, reefs and points waiting for surfers to discover. The Highlands of Scotland have some of the best reef breaks in Europe – at Thurso and Brimms Ness. Along the East coast waves break from the tip of Scotland to the Norfolk coast which have mostly remained unridden. In the south the channel coast gets storm surf and it is not unusual to see people surfing the beach breaks at Brighton and Littlehamp-

ton in the depths of winter.

Because there is a severe winter in Britain the best surfing months are May, September and October. The summer months of June and July tend to be flat with only the occasional swell. The sport is becoming more and more popular each year. The southwest areas, Devon and Cornwall, have the best waves and plenty of facilities for buying boards and wetsuits. British waves are predominantly beach breaks with the odd reef and point break. Visitors to Britain are surprised at the size and quality of the waves. Because of frequent Atlantic storms the coastline has consistent swells in Spring, Autumn and Winter when the low pressure areas track up the western approaches. Britain's best wave is at Porthleen, Cornwall, which is a right-hand reef break that, on ideal swell and tide conditions, becomes cylindrical, presenting the rider with deep tube rides.

SOUTH AFRICA

A politically-charged area that has had an effect on all sports, though surfing has come out relatively unscathed. South Africa hosts two "A"-rated ASP World Tour events and the majority of professional surfers compete in South Africa although some boycott the events. For a surfing trip South Africa has a lot to offer. The legendary Jefferies

Bay has a reputation of being one of the world's most demanding waves to ride with many critical sections. The hub of South Africa surfing is Durban with many fine surfing beaches such as the Bay of Plenty, and Dairy Beach. If you are planning a trip to South Africa, Durban is a good starting point to buy a surfboard and get acclimatized before heading off on a surfing safari to Jefferies Bay, Seal point and cape St. Francis. The South Africans have produced some world-class surfers such as Shaun Tomson, Martin Potter, and Mike Burness. Try to plan your trip around the ASP contest leaving yourself time to see these surfers in action.

HAWAII

The North Shore of Hawaii is the testing ground for surfers and equipment. From November to February such famous breaks as Pipeline, Sunset and Waimea Bay are pounded by massive Pacific swells. The top surfers in the world travel to these islands to surf the huge waves, but the average surfer will feel content with the less intense waves on the South Shore which break at other times of the year. Hawaii has the reputation of being a "locals-only" place and on some beaches the locals are openly hostile to outsiders. Hawaii is a place where you have to buy your equipment. It is quite expensive but the

THE ASP WORLD TOUR "A"-RATED EVENTS

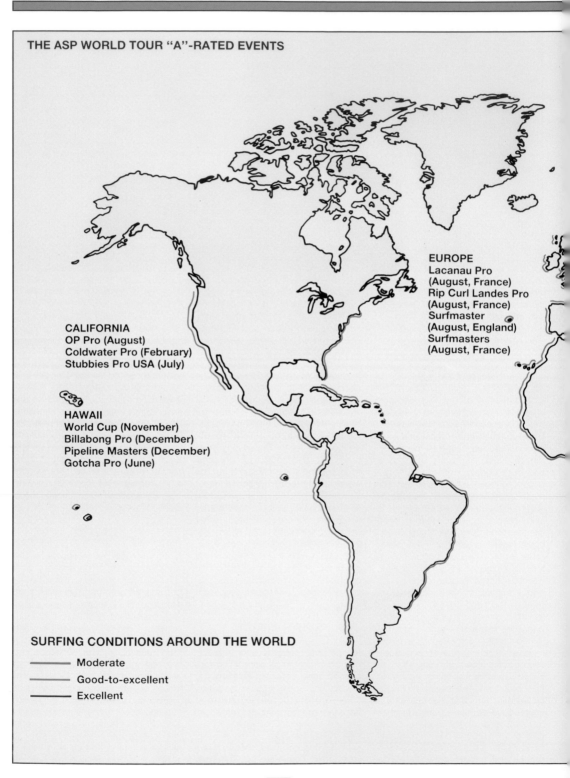

EUROPE
Lacanau Pro
(August, France)
Rip Curl Landes Pro
(August, France)
Surfmaster
(August, England)
Surfmasters
(August, France)

CALIFORNIA
OP Pro (August)
Coldwater Pro (February)
Stubbies Pro USA (July)

HAWAII
World Cup (November)
Billabong Pro (December)
Pipeline Masters (December)
Gotcha Pro (June)

SURFING CONDITIONS AROUND THE WORLD

—— Moderate
—— Good-to-excellent
—— Excellent

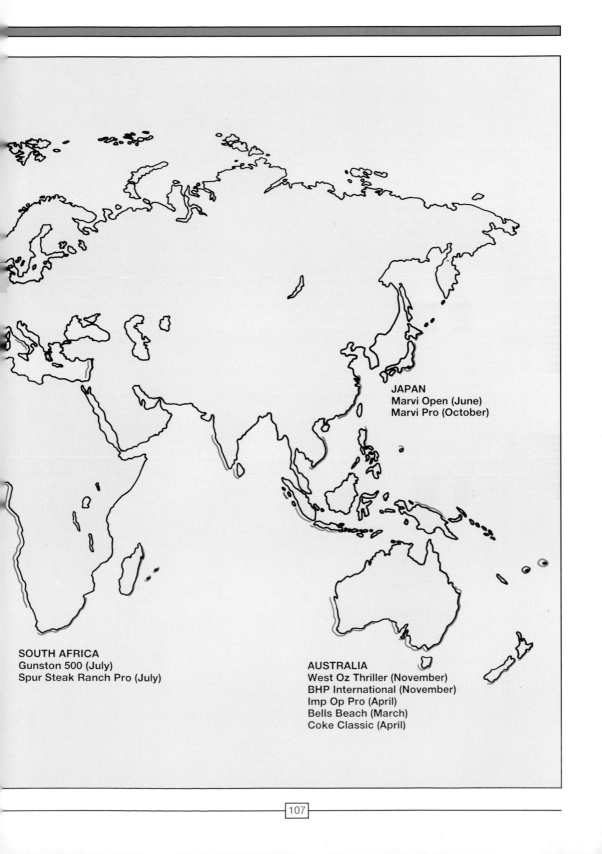

JAPAN
Marvi Open (June)
Marvi Pro (October)

SOUTH AFRICA
Gunston 500 (July)
Spur Steak Ranch Pro (July)

AUSTRALIA
West Oz Thriller (November)
BHP International (November)
Imp Op Pro (April)
Bells Beach (March)
Coke Classic (April)

boards are made for the specific wave conditions in the islands.

If you are a committed surfer and have ridden what you consider to be big waves wait until you go to Hawaii. Waves you considered to be huge are half the size of the ones on the Hawaiian scale! Certain waves do not even break below 3 metres (6 feet). The North Shore annually claims the lives of surfers who are unaware of the awesome power of Hawaiian waves. Many good surfers have experienced the most hideous wipeouts at Sunset and Pipeline being driven into the sea bed by huge walls of breaking water. I have heard it said that if you could harness the power of a 10 metre (30 feet) Waimea Bay wave it would keep the lights glowing on the north shore for 15 minutes.

Above: Brazil, the South Americans are making an impact on the professional surfing scene, staging high prize money contests annually.

Below: Hans Hedeman, Hawaii. The islands break best between December and February. The top surfers in the world visit Hawaii to ride the north shore.

AUSTRALIA

This is the largest island on earth, populated mostly around the coastal regions. Australia has excellent surf from Perth to Brisbane, with the most crowded areas being around the Sydney suburbs and on Queensland's Gold Coast. If you are planning to take a trip to Australia you will have to pick a specific area

Left: Mike Parons in California. Though crowded the standard of surfing is extremely high and competition to get waves is fierce.

Below: Bobby Owen, Bell Beach, Victoria, Australia. Bell's is the big wave area, and the annual Easter ASP contest is the high spot of the tour here.

to visit. The continent is so vast it would take a lifetime to surf all the breaks. The Pacific Coast Highway which runs from Sydney to Brisbane is a good route to follow. It takes in all the famous breaks of north Sydney into New South Wales and Queensland. Most surfers fly into one of the major cities such as Perth, Melbourne, Sydney or Brisbane. There is little need to take a surfboard or wetsuit to Australia, the coastal towns are all populated with surfers and there are literally hundreds of surf shops and factories.

The Australians are a somewhat forthright race, rarely tolerating fouls in the water. So if you drop in on an Aussie be prepared to be verbally abused. If you want relatively uncrowded waves the surf around Victoria is the place. Alternatively, if you want life in the fast-lane Sydney, the Gold Coast, or Surfer's Paradise are the places to go. Australia offers the average surfers a selection of waves from moderate to excellent. The climate is ideally suited for surfing. Wetsuits are worn on overcast winter days and in the

Below: Darren Potter at Fistral Beach, Newquay, England. The best time to visit England for waves like this is in April and May, or September and October.

Bottom: Jim Hogan, Durban City Surf at Dairy Beach. Durban has excellent beach and reef breaks. Equipment is plentiful from the city's many surf shops.

Above: Kuta Reef, Bali. 90° under clear blue skies, surfers hitch a ride out to the reef – tropical paradise. The only unfriendly things are the sea snakes!

southern state of Victoria, but in nothern New South Wales and Queensland it is definitely a shorts-only climate.

USA

California is the birthplace of modern surfing and the hotbed of all that is happening in the surfing world. This is the image portrayed by US surfing magazines. What they do not tell you is that all the major surf breaks in California are so crowded at most times of the year

all along the coast so that surfing has almost become a team sport!

There is also good surfing in Oregon, Mexico, Texas, Florida and all the way up the East Coast to New York State. It would take a lifetime to get around them all. If you are planning a trip to the USA then study the area carefully.

If you decide to go to a major surfing centre then buy a surfboard there. Do not risk having problems by carrying a board with you. As I said earlier if your board is not designed for the local type of waves. Nobody is going to be too keen to buy it off you or trade it in. This is something that works in reverse if you buy a board in the USA and take it home, you will probably get more for it than you paid for it in American so you can recoup your money.

INDONESIA

The tropical island of Bali is the best known surfing location since it was discovered in the early 70s. Most famous of the island's breaks are Ulawata and Padang Padang. To get around Bali you need to hire a motorbike or car; without transport you are limited to surfing and staying on one of the beach breaks such as Kuta. A good selection of secondhand surfboards are available at Ulawata but I would suggest that you take a board with you if you intend to ride the barrelling tubes of Ulawata and Padang Padang, then you will need a longer big wave board as well as a board for smaller beach break waves. There are other more remote islands not as crowded as Bali such as Lombok

and Java which are as exotic.

The island of Java is in fact just starting to be opened up as a surfing location. As a starting point for an Indonesian surf trip and to acclimatize I would suggest Bali as your first destination so that you get used to the juicier waves, tropical heat and

TAKING YOUR BOARD

There is no worse feeling on earth than falling down the face of a pitching 15ft (5 metres) monster on your "hot dog" board. If you choose to travel to a destination that has a specific type of wave that requires specialist equipment, consider the option of buying a board when you get there if it is a once in a lifetime trip to Hawaii or Australia. Don't cut corners by taking your own board, the odds are it won't be suitable for juicy waves.

American Jeff Novak in the slot,
Grand Plage, Biarritz, France.

the great number of sea snakes.

You could take in Bali as a stop-over en-route to Australia as now some airlines offer incredible package deals on this route, taking in also Fiji and Hawaii with a possible stopover in Los Angeles.

BRAZIL

Rio de Janeiro is the capital of South America surfing, hosting an ASP World Tour event. I am told by the surfers on the world tour that what Rio lacks in waves it makes up for in fiestas! Brazil is emerging as the major surfing force in Central and South America. They have competing surfers on both the amateur and professional scene.

A trip to Brazil can be expensive but once there a surfer can start to discover other South American countries such as Costa Rica, Venezuela, Uruguay, Peru and Ecuador. From reports by surfers who have been to South America it seems an ideal location for a surf safari.

SURF SAFARI

The ultimate surfing trip is the surf safari – a trip of discovery to surf waves that have rarely, if ever, been surfed before. There is a lot of planning necessary if you decide to go on safari as I found out when I went

on a special surf safari to the Canary Islands with top European surfers Grishka Roberts and Peter Lascelles.

On a safari it is not like jetting off to Australia or the US because we had to take all our equipment with us. We flew from London not knowing if our boards had even been put on the plane. The airline had surprised us at the last moment by say-

Above: Uluwatu, Bali. The islands of Indonesia such as Bali are well known but there remain others where surfing has still only got a tentative toe-hold.

Below: Peter Lascelles checks that the surfboards are strapped on securely before we start the search for waves on the volcanic island of Lanzarote.

ing they may have to follow two days later!

Upon landing at Fuerteventura we found that Peter, an Australian, needed a visa to get into the islands whereas Grishka and myself did not. From the start our plans had become unstuck; no surfboards and minus one surfer. After two hours of argument and bargaining Peter was allowed into the islands. Minutes later we saw the surfboards being unceremoniously dropped from the plane on to the runway below, followed closely by the bag that contained my camera equipment!

Reunited with our equipment we went in search of the jeep. From Fuerteventura we took the ferry to Lanzarote. As the crossing was quite rough we had a fair idea that there would be waves at our destination. What we did not know was that we were about to experience a rare set of circumstances that would produce waves of a size and quality more often found in Hawaii.

Lanzarote is not the most scenic of places. Over the centuries volcanos have erupted frequently, spilling

vast amounts of lava across the landscape. In fact, the island is one big lava field broken only by the volcanos towering out of the black waste.

On previous visits to the island I had heard stories about two bays that only broke in extremely rare occasions when the swell was in a particular northerly direction. It was these two as yet unridden and

Above: In the quest for unridden waves, we searched the remote North-west tip of Lanzarote in the Oanary Islands by jeep. We were rewarded at "Thirty".

Below: The bay was protected from the wind by a headland and the right looked to be the best wave to ride. We wondered how many surfers had ridden it.

Left: This a righthand peak formed perfectly over the volcanic reef. However, it broke onto a headland.

unphotographed bays that we had come to surf. I had a rough map of the area given to me on my previous trip some years back.

Once off the main track our jeep was put to some hard driving. We could see heavy lines marching in from the horizon even at this distance so the surf looked very big. Picking our way through the terrain down to the coast there was a buzz of excitement and a great deal of speculation as to the size and qual-ity of the waves. Our jeep pulled into a small village of some two dozen white houses. In front of the small harbour was a reef with 1.5 metre (4 feet) lefts forming and peeling off perfectly, but over the other side of the bay was a much bigger right-hand peak that was running out of deep water up the reef. The waves peeled off breaking in the same place each time. The wave looked easy on take off but there was a criti-cal tubing section that broke close to the jagged volcanic cliff face. After studying the wave for half an hour Grishka Roberts and Peter Lascelles paddled out to attempt to ride this previously unsurfed wave. They had weighed up the danger; they were unaware of the depth of water the wave broke in. What they did know was the reef was made of razor sharp volcanic lava that on dry land could not be walked on bare-foot. Grishka took off on the first wave, dropping in to write another sentence in the history of surfing. Being the first to ride the wave he was allowed the honour of naming it, calling it simply, "Thirty."

Below: The island's backdrop was barren and eerie with nobody around for miles. The surfers had to exercise caution in case of a bad wipeout.

FINALLY, THE BASIC RULES FOR ALL SURFERS

The surfer on the inside has the right of way
The surfer on the inside against the peak has the unconditional right of way. It is his wave; never attempt to take off or drop in on him.

Be aware of other surfers
At all times always consider the safety of other surfers in close proximity to you.

Never abandon your surfboard
In a crowded surfing area keep control of your surfboard at all times. Do not jump off when faced with a possible collision.

Never throw away your surfboard
To avoid the battering action of a wave always keep a tight grip on your board.

If you lose your board
If your board is wrenched from your grip try to catch hold of the leash at a point as near to the board as possible. This will minimise the amount of distance the board will travel.

Other water users
When you are on a wave be aware of other water users who are unfamiliar with these basic rules: boogie boarders and wave-ski riders.

Left: Grishka Roberts picks his way barefoot over the razor sharp volcanic rock. He had to wait between sets to paddle out to the peak.

Below: Grishka took off on the first wave; the sneaker sets kept catching the surface inside. The break proved highly unpredictable.

GLOSSARY

Aerial an extremely difficult airbourne manoeuvre that involves the surfer launching off the lip of the wave at high speed and, in theory, landing again. Top Pro Martin Potter is the leading exponent of this move.

Axed being hit by the falling lip of the wave and wiped out.

Backhand surfing with one's back to the wave face.

Barrel hollow, tubing section of a wave.

Beach break waves breaking over sand.

Blank a large block of foam from which a surfboard is shaped.

Bottom turn the first turn of the ride, at the bottom of the wave face (see page 44).

Close-out a wave that breaks all the way along its length simultaneously, without peeling. Bad news.

Custom board a surfboard shaped specifically to the customer's requirements.

Cutback a turning manoeuvre on the shoulder of the wave that carries the surfer back into the pocket of the wave.

Deck the upper surface of the board.

Delamination a defective condition where the fibreglass skin of a board has become unbonded from the inner foam core.

Ding a dent or hole in a surfboard. This should be temporarily covered with tape to prevent water-logging, and repaired as soon as possible.

Drop, to take the to launch from the peak of the wave and drop down the face. When the wave is steep or big, "taking the drop" is often a matter of critical timing and requires considerable nerve on the part of the surfer.

Drop in when one surfer takes off on a wave that is already being ridden by another surfer who is nearer the curl. Considered bad wave etiquette, although sometimes unintentional.

Forehand surfing with one's front to the wave. A natural-footed surfer rides a right-hand wave on his forehand.

Floater re-entry, or "floater" Difficult manoeuvre, a variation on the standard re-entry that involves launching the board off the lip of the wave, unweighting, and free-falling back down with the curtain of white-water.

Glassy smooth almost oily look to waves when wind conditions are dead calm. Most common in the morning or evening, they are great for surfing.

"Gnarly" slang term used to describe large, heavy, thick-lipped, or difficult waves.

Goofy-foot, or "goofy" a surfer who stands on his board with his right foot forward.

Gun a long, narrow, spear-shaped board specifically designed for riding big waves.

Hang five a manoeuvre that involves dangling the five toes of the front foot over the nose of the board. A common part of a proficient longboarder's repertoire, sometimes possible on a shortboard.

Hang ten a difficult variation of the above – and only possible on a longboard – when the surfer hangs the toes of both feet over the nose of the board while cruising along the wave.

Hollow a steep and concave wave-face shape.

Impact zone the area of a break between the line-up and the shore where the waves break the hardest. Not a good place to hang around for very long.

Interference competition term for a drop-in. The surfer who commits an interference will be penalised by the judges; the surfer dropped-in on will probably break the other guy's legs when the heat is over.

Kick-out a controlled method of ending a ride by turning the board up the face and over the top of the wave ahead of the curl.

Leash thin cord made of stretchy urethane which attaches a surfer to his or her board.

Left-hander, or "left" a wave that breaks towards the left when viewed from the line-up.

Line-up the area just outside the break where the surfers sit and wait for set waves.

Lip the crest or top of the wave,

which – when the waves are hollow – can throw out to form a tube.

Malibu board long, rounded surfboard used by longboarders.

Moulded board, or "pop out" a mass-produced surfboard made by injecting foam into a mould. Cheaper and more hard wearing than a custom board.

"Maxed out" when a break cannot cope with or "hold" a large swell; the waves will usually close out or break erratically. Even Waimea Bay in Hawaii (where the biggest waves in the world are ridden) get maxed out at 35 feet.

Natural foot a surfer who stands on his board with his left foot forward.

Nose the front or pointed end of the surfboard.

Offshore wind, or "offshore" a wind blowing out to sea at 90° to the incoming waves, tending to hold them up and make them more hollow. A light offshore with a decent swell usually means superb surfing conditions.

Off-the-lip, or off-the-top immensely satisfying manoeuvre when the board is smashed off the lip of the wave, just ahead of the curl.

Onshore wind, or "onshore" a wind blowing from the sea straight towards the shore. Tends to make paddling out difficult, spoils the shape of the waves, and causes chop. In other words, bad news.

Out the back, or "outside" the area beyond the impact zone, where the waves are forming but not quite breaking. When someone in the line-up shouts "Outside!" it means that there's a big set on its way so paddle farther out.

"Over the falls" invigorating, unintentional, and sometimes disastrous descent down the wave face inside the falling lip.

Peak the highest part of the wave which usually jacks up and breaks first.

Pocket the part of the wave face just ahead of the curl, where the wave is steepest.

Point break a surf break where the waves wrap around a point or headland and peel off continuously.

Prone position lying face down on the board with one's head toward its nose.

Priority competition term used when one surfer has precedence and choice of wave, usually because he has paddled around a "priority" marker buoy.

Pumping when the waves at a break are working really well.

Pumping the board method of increasing one's speed across the wave face by "working" the board while it is trimmed.

Quiver a set or selection of surfboards, of slightly different lengths and shapes, to suit different types of wave.

Radical, or "rad" slang term used to describe an exciting or outrageous manoeuvre performed by a surfer.

Rail the edge of a surfboard.

Reef break waves breaking over an offshore reef of rock or coral; the most famous reefbreak in the world is Pipeline in Hawaii.

Re-entry, or "reo" difficult manoeuvre carried out on, over, or off the breaking lip of the wave.

"Rhino chaser" a long gun, used for tackling the very largest of all waves.

Right-hander, or "right" a wave that breaks towards the right when viewed from the line-up.

Rip current, or "rip" a strong, often dangerous, current that flows from the impact zone out to sea.

Rollercoaster a manoeuvre that involves riding over the white-water that has broken and spilled down the wave face.

Rocker the curve along the length of a surfboard; measured by shapers along the bottom surface.

Suction a part of a wave which breaks in a specific way repeatedly: for example a bowl section, or a close-out section.

Set a group or pack of larger waves.

Shaper a usually deaf and dust-covered person who can carve a perfect surfboard shape out of a big chunk of foam in a matter of seconds.

Shoulder the sloping part of the wave face ahead of the pocket, where cutback manoeuvres are performed.

Sneaker set, clean-up set a group of much larger-than-normal waves that come through every once in a while and catch most people napping.

Soup the white-water of a wave that has already broken.

Spin out sideways motion of board as it loses contact with the wave face during the drop or bottom turn; usually results in a wipeout.

Streamer a full wetsuit with long arms and long legs.

Stringer the central strip of wood that runs down the middle of the board.

Sucky when a wave is intense, thick-lipped and hollow, often because it is breaking in shallow water.

Switch-foot an adept surfer who can ride waves both natural-footed and goofy-footed.

Tail the rear, fin end of the surfboard.

Take-off the start of a ride, ideally from the peak of the wave.

Trimming the board to adjust one's weight and stance so that the board planes at the maximum possible speed.

Tube the inside of a cylindrical, barrelling wave.

Wax is to stop you skating!

White-water the frothy turbulent water of the part of the wave that has already broken.

Wipeout to crash or fall off your board.

Vee the convex curve or shape across the bottom of the board from rail to rail.

Zinc cream, or "zinc" opaque water-proof cream applied to the nose, lips, and cheeks in order to prevent sunburn; usually white, some coloured brands are now available.

INTERNATIONAL SURFING ASSOCIATIONS

AUSTRALIA
Australian Surfriding Association
2b Anderson Street
Torquay 3228
Victoria AUSTRALIA

GREAT BRITAIN
British Surfing Association
G5 Burrows Chambers
East Burrow Road
Swansea SA1 1RF
West Glamorgan UK

FRANCE
Federation Francois de Surf
BP-28 Plage Nord
40150 Hossegor FRANCE

HAWAII
Hawaiian Surfing Association
PO Box 4560
Honolulu
Hawaii 96812 USA

JAPAN
Nipon Surfing Association
Ochanomizu KS Building 403
3-3-1 Hongo Bunkyo-Ku
Tokyo 113 JAPAN

NEW ZEALAND
New Zealand Surfriders
Association
PO Box 1026
Gisborne NEW ZEALAND

USA
United States Surfing Federation
11 Adam Point Road
Barrington
Rhode Island 02806 USA

FURTHER READING

British Surfing Association. (1988). *A Guide to Surfing in Britain.*

Channon and McLeod. (1986). *Surfing Wild Australia.* Surfing World Publications, Australia.

Channon and McLeod. (1987). *Surfing the Ring of Fire.* Surfing World Publications, Australia.

London. (1988). *Competitive Surfing – A Dedicated Approach.* Mouvement Publications, Australia.

Wavelength. Published monthly. Unity Hall, Cleveden Road, Newquay, Cornwall, TR7 2BU, England.

INDEX

Numbers in *italics* refer to illustrations

SURFERS AND LOCATIONS

PHOTOGRAPHIC ACKNOWLEDGEMENTS

John Conway/Canon 10, 15-9, 21, 23-5, 28-1, 33-47, 49, 52-3, 55, 58, 60-3, 65-7, 72-5, 78-9, 84-7, 94-105, 114-7, 127; Guy Finlay 81; Paul Maartens 110; Ocean Pacific 88; Peter Simons 56, 109; Peter Wilson 80, 108

PRINTED IN BELGIUM BY
proost
INTERNATIONAL BOOK PRODUCTION